MW00647395

I SLEEP AROUND

THE HUMOROUS MEMOIR OF A NOMADIC WRITER

SUE ANN JAFFARIAN

I SLEEP AROUND: THE HUMOROUS MEMOIR OF A NOMADIC
WRITER

ISBN: 978-1-963705-96-6

Published in the United States of America by Harbor Lane Books, LLC.

www.harborlanebooks.com

For Todd and Shari Swanson.
Thank you from the bottom of my heart.
Without your generous support, this crazy adventure would
never have gotten off the ground.

Special Dedication

For Dawn Dowdle, my agent who recognized the potential in
this book, but unexpectedly passed away before seeing it
come to fruition.

THE ROAD IS CALLING
BY SUE ANN JAFFARIAN

The road is calling and I must go.
No longer content to sit.
No longer happy being rooted.
Sticks and bricks no longer hold me.
Material things no longer entice.

The road is calling, subtle, seductive.
It fills my ears with tales of new places.
Beckons me with promises of new people.
Woos me with new tastes and smells.
Taunts me with the waiting unknown.

The road is calling, like a sexy lover.
Tantalizing me with new experiences.
Whispering about new adventures.
Embracing me with miles of comfort.
Life is waiting for me. On the road.

INTRODUCTION

No matter who you are, living on the road changes you. It cannot be helped. The experiences you have, the different people you meet, and the challenges you face all work together to mold and shape you, like a clay pot turning on a potter's wheel. As I pen this book, I am changed from when I began this journey. Not a different person, but I'd like to think that I'm a better version of myself.

Traveling through the country via roads instead of on airplanes forces you to slow down and see people and places up close and personal, both the good and the not so good. It also forces you to get to know yourself up close and personal, both the good and the not so good. Living full-time on the road ejects you out of your comfort zone. Not just once, but over and over until it becomes the norm. Until you come to expect and even welcome it.

The change does not happen overnight. You simply don't begin a journey of this type and the next day—*boom!*—you're different. It's a slow change, rather like a meandering river that winds around bends with low-hanging trees dripping with Spanish moss, including the occasional chiggers.

At some point during your journey, you realize it. And when it happens, you might find yourself rather surprised. There's no set time frame for this. It could happen a month into traveling, six months, or a few years, but at some point you will realize that the changes in you finally caught up with the big change you made in your lifestyle.

Living full-time on the road in a recreational vehicle (RV) is not for everyone. Not everyone has positive experiences stemming from it. Most of my experiences have been very positive, with a few glitches here and there. I love this lifestyle. It feels as if I have finally discovered the road—or many roads—I was destined to travel.

Before I took to the open road as a lifestyle, I read three books about road travel:

Travels With Charley by John Steinbeck

Blue Highways by William Least Heat-Moon

Nomadland by Jessica Bruder

I found *Travels With Charley* charming but a bit romanticized. The other two books were much more realistic. All were, and still are, worth reading. *Blue Highways* was my favorite of the three. It urged me to get off interstates and seek out small towns along lesser traveled roads. It's something I still do years later. *Nomadland* was the most heartbreaking, and is now an excellent hit movie. It mostly tells of people forced to take to the road because of financial hardship or other personal reasons. That was not my case, or the case of many of my friends who are also living full-time on the road. Our reasons are much more about learning and experiencing new things.

Every mile I've driven, every person I've met, and everything I've seen has changed me in some way. The United States is stunningly beautiful. I've seen things that have left me gobsmacked, like Carlsbad Caverns, The Grand Tetons reflected in a lake, the Badlands of South Dakota, and the Badlands of North Dakota. I've met people so different from me, yet so kind and interesting. There were some who were not that gracious, but they were definitely in the minority. I've seen fun things that gave me a greater appreciation of the quirky side of life. I've seen bison, elk, alligators, wild turkeys, armadillos, numerous deer, and donkeys. I have become familiar with different species of birds. One of my greatest pleasures was watching a bald eagle take flight from the ground just a few yards from me. Often, these animals were on the road. I've had to exercise patience, coupled with great awe, while they held up traffic before moseying along their way.

Almost every day, I learn something new about a place, history, people, or even myself.

This book, *I Sleep Around*, is the story of the first two years of my journey and on-the-road education, as well as the planning it took to make this happen. Originally, the book was going to cover only my first year of travel. Then, three months into my second year, while I was working on this book, the coronavirus pandemic hit, totally changing how people traveled and interacted with each other. Those of us living on the road full-time were nearly orphaned. When that happened, I knew I could not write a book about my first year and be done with it. I had to also chronicle the pandemic's impact on my journey, itinerary, and life.

I hope this book inspires readers to follow their own dreams, whether it be RVing or something else entirely.

SECTION ONE

A NEW WAY OF LIVING

"If people aren't laughing at your dreams, your dreams aren't big enough!"
— **Robin S. Sharma**

AN RV? SERIOUSLY?

As I go from town to town, sleeping wherever I can park my van, telling people about my journey and my books, I can't help but think I am becoming carny folk.

I wrote the above words on Facebook on October 30, 2019, at the end of my tenth month as a full-time van traveler. As I posted those words, I was sitting at a picnic table in North Carolina. The next day I would be giving another presentation at another library. I had spoken at many libraries and at some non-library events all over the country already, with many more on my schedule.

It was a warm, fall day, slightly windy. Ringing the perimeter of the rest area were trees dressed in the gold and copper of fall. I was happy, yet pensive. Soon, I would be celebrating one year on the road, traveling the country, and living full-time in a 2016 Winnebago Travato 59K, a Class B RV. It's a twenty-foot van with less than one hundred square feet of living space, complete with a galley and a bathroom with a shower. Before the night was over, I'd be bedding down in the parking lot of a Cracker Barrel restaurant in South Carolina. Not my first night at a Cracker Barrel, or sleeping in a parking lot. Nor would it be my last.

In preparation for life on the road, I retired from my very long career as a corporate paralegal. I turned sixty-six in December of 2018, and retired from the law firm I'd been working at for almost thirteen years a week later. There was a small retirement party with my friends the next day. The day after that, I sold my car. On December 31, 2018, I took to the road as a full-time nomadic writer, leaving my life in California behind forever.

Many people are surprised to learn that I was never a camper. Not ever. I didn't camp with my family growing up or as an adult. Except for the occasional summer camp as a kid, I had gone camping exactly once in my life, in my early twenties. It was tent camping with friends and definitely not for me. I had never spent time in an RV at all. Nor am I very outdoorsy. When I began this, I was as outdoorsy as chintz curtains. Now, I consider myself as outdoorsy as a picnic table—sturdy, stable, and outside, but still not ready to hike steep trails or overgrown paths, or kayak rivers and streams. You might say I am outdoorsy-lite.

So why did I choose to retire and take to the road in a van-size RV if I'd never done this before? Trust me, a lot of my friends asked me this often. Some are still asking, though fewer as time goes on.

About three years before I retired, I started looking at retirement options. I took into account different cities and states and types of housing available. Although I would be a retired paralegal, I wouldn't be retired from my productive writing career. The beauty of writing is that I could and do write anywhere. Many friends suggested their towns for my golden years. My family rooted for New England. I didn't have a specific place in mind. I didn't care if it got cold where I relocated as long as it was not super cold. I wasn't wild about desert summers, either. I also wanted a place that was convenient to an airport because I wanted to travel after retirement.

One thing became clear during my research. As long as I chose my location wisely, I could purchase or rent a decent place to live when I retired, but I wouldn't have a lot of money left over for extensive travel. Travel would be possible, but not as much as I wanted. Regrouping was in order.

I did more research. This time, I researched retirement options, not just locations. I know people who retired to other less expensive countries, but that didn't interest me. Some friends shared homes with other retirees to cut costs. That sounded interesting, but I wasn't on board with that idea yet. Then, I stumbled across the idea of living in an RV.

Wait! People really do this? Tell me more!

I started reading every article and blog on full-time RVing, particularly those from people around my age. I watched hundreds of YouTube videos on the subject, including how to dump and maintain your onboard sewer system and do minor repairs. I learned how to get mail, medical help, and how to find inexpensive camping. Would I prefer staying in RV parks for a month at a time? Or would I rather go from place to place like, well, carny folk? I studied it all and made a checklist that served me well later.

The more I read and researched, the more I knew this was what I wanted to do, or at least try. I could have a home and the ability to travel, all wrapped up together. It simply felt right. Then, I had a dream that solidified it for me. In the dream, I was sitting in an RV at a table, writing away. I had the door open and through it I could see trees and a light rain falling. More importantly, I felt at peace and

4 SUE ANN JAFFARIAN

happier than I had ever been. This might sound screwy to some, but having that dream was really when I knew this was the right path for me. Since then, I have often been in my RV with the sliding door open, writing away while surrounded by nature, and sometimes even with a light rain falling. And you know what? I am always happy and content when I'm doing that. My dream came true.

When I started telling people I wanted to live full-time in a van, many laughed. Out loud. In my face. Years before, people laughed when I told them I was going to write a book. Over thirty books later, no one is laughing, unless it's because they read a funny passage in one of my books. As with writing, many thought it was just some cockamamie idea that I would soon kick to the curb. A few friends were worried that I would be homeless. Some still think of me as homeless.

O ye of little faith!

There were those who mulled it over, then decided it sounded like fun and very doable. Those were the people I clung to for encouragement, not the naysayers. I didn't need people peeing on my parade. But even if all had been negative on the idea, I still would have pushed ahead because, frankly, I'm pigheaded. If I hit a roadblock, I would go around it. If a bridge went out, I would build another. I would only stop if something occurred that was a clear-cut sign that I should not go forward with this idea. And there *were* road closures and crumbled bridges along the way.

It seemed like the perfect solution. I would have a home that would also allow me to travel. I could write on the road and about the road. I could visit libraries and readers all over the country. Once the idea of retirement in an RV was firm in my mind, I set out to find the perfect RV for me.

I also rented an RV for several days, just to see if I really wanted to do this. At the time, members of my family would camp in the fall in Rhode Island. I couldn't find a van to rent, instead renting a Class C from Cruise America in Connecticut and driving it to the campground in Rhode Island. I highly recommend doing this if you're not that familiar with RVs. It's a good way to get a feel for them. During this time, I did my first dump, first hookups, showered, and cooked. Everything went great. I spent five days in it and learned two major things:

   1) I enjoyed the lifestyle and being in the RV;

   2) I did not want a Class C or larger.

RVs basically have three classifications: Class As are the big bus-like RVs; Class Bs are the van-style RVs, also known as camper vans; and Class Cs are the more traditional RVs, usually with a sleeping or storage area over the cab. There are also travel trailers to consider, known as towables.

Early on, I was enchanted by the idea of a Class B RV. I wanted one of the slick vans, which would be more manageable, smaller, easy to drive and park, and better on gas. I researched the different models and manufacturers and went to a couple of RV shows and dealerships to look at them. From the beginning, the Winnebago Travato caught my eye, mostly because the floor plan was more to my liking. I really disliked the Class B models with the bathroom in the middle of the van. As I told one RV salesman, I didn't want the ability to use the toilet and make breakfast at the same time. The Travato 59G had a good-sized bathroom off to the rear side. However, when I went to see one in person, I was disappointed. Not in the van. It was pretty spectacular. The problem was that the bed and some of the features were built very high, and I am very short. I was worried that over time I might injure myself trying to get in and out of that high bed. After all, I was in my sixties at the time and sometimes needed to get up during the night. Now that I'm in my early seventies, I am really happy I made that decision. I went back to looking at other Class B and smaller Class C RVs, but my heart still belonged to the Travato. At that time, I joined a fairly new group on Facebook called *Travato Owners and Wannabees (TOAW)*, a group for people who either owned or wanted to own a Travato. It's now a huge group, as the popularity of this vehicle has exploded over the past several years. I also joined a couple of other Facebook groups for other RV models to learn more about them from actual owners.

Then, one day I was scouting vans online and saw that Winnebago had released a new model of Travato. It was a 59K with twin beds and a more open floor plan. It was a total game changer for me. I learned as much as I could about it and eventually found one at a local RV dealership. I wasn't ready to buy one yet since I still had a couple of years before retirement, but I wanted to check out this new model.

I was smitten! I could reach everything. The bathroom was in the back and large for a van. There was no dinette table, but there was a pullout table I could use as a dining table and desk. As soon as I stepped into the van, it felt like home.

The next year, I went to the big RV show in Pomona and checked it out again, along with other models I still had my eye on. Once again, I looked at various Class B models and a few of the smaller Class C ones. Both Travato models were there side by side so I could compare them. I stuck around the Travato display much of the afternoon and visited with other people from the Facebook group. I was already a big fan of Stefany and James Adinaro of The Fit RV. I had started following their videos and blog when I first got the idea of living in an RV. They were there, and they welcomed me. I went all fan girl. I also met Russ Garfin, an executive with Winnebago, and other representatives. I took the opportunity to ask a ton of questions.

If you're looking to buy an RV, do your homework. Do not impulse buy. It's easy to do, especially when a dealer is smooth talking in your ear and offering killer deals. I'm convinced that a lot of disgruntled RV owners purchased the wrong RV for their needs. Go to shows and check out a lot of makes and models. Sit in them for whatever time it takes. Open cabinets, pretend you're washing dishes, making the bed, or using the bathroom. Do not be shy and don't let a salesperson rush you. Make a list of your must-haves, but be prepared to compromise on a few things.

When I first began looking at RVs, my must-haves were totally different than when I finally decided on a vehicle. At first, my main must-have was a dry bath, a bathroom where the shower and toilet are separate. Once I fell in love with the Class B vans, I cast that must-have aside and accepted the wet bath, a bathroom where the shower is in the toilet area. That compromise allowed me to embrace the RV I really wanted and needed. I have never regretted my decision.

If you're thinking of getting an RV, know exactly what you want and need before pulling out your checkbook. Better yet, leave your checkbook, debit card, and credit cards at home when you're first looking at RVs. When you're ready to buy, get referrals for dealers from other RVers. Do not go to a place just because they are close to you. I ended up buying used from a private individual I trusted, but many of my friends bought RVs hundreds and even thousands of miles away from their homes because of the good reputations and deals of certain dealers.

I SLEEP AROUND

There are times when I wake up in the morning and have no idea where I am. And, no, alcohol is not involved. I'm in my van, of course, but geographically confused. Am I in a Walmart, a rest stop, a casino or truck stop parking lot? A campground? In the boonies? An RV park? In a darkened van early in the morning, all locations look alike until you raise a shade. Even once the shade is up, sometimes I will wonder what state, town, or even time zone I'm in.

This gives real meaning to the common RVing phrase, *home is where you park it*. I even have a pillow with that on it, given to me by a friend. I am home wherever I park my tiny house on wheels. Everything I own is in it. My van is like a nurturing parent. It carries me. Cleans me up. Feeds me. Gives me a place to sleep.

The first night I owned my Travato, which I named *Novella*, I slept in the Walmart parking lot in Greer, South Carolina. This practice is tagged Wallydocking (Walmart + boondocking or dry camping). I had purchased my RV from a man who lived in South Carolina and was a member of the Travato group. I'd flown in from Los Angeles, California, to pick it up. He gave me a thorough tutorial on the features of the van, and then I left his home, determined to get on the road heading west. I was still working at the time and needed to get back to Los Angeles as soon as possible. There would be no time for sightseeing or recreational camping.

I chose Walmart for my inaugural overnight for two reasons:

1) It was a free overnight spot;

2) I needed to outfit the van with some basics like bedding and food. All I had brought with me were some clothing, toiletries, and a camping towel and facecloth. Technically, the overnight spot was not free. It cost me over three hundred dollars. What surprised me was how well I slept. After a red-eye to South Carolina, learning about the van, buying supplies, and then setting up the inside, I was exhausted. You would think I'd be a little apprehensive, but I wasn't.

My first shower in the van was the next morning in the Walmart parking lot. It felt really weird taking that first shower. In my van, the bathroom is across the back, just a metal door away from people and vehicles coming and going. Yet, there I was, wet, naked, and very vulnerable. I always make sure my doors are locked when I'm in the van, so no one is going to yank open those doors and expose me. But it still felt unsettling the first few times I showered inside it. It was the same with using my bathroom in parking lots and pull-outs along the highway. The first few times, you feel rather exposed, like you're about to be caught with your pants down, literally. Like everything else, you get used to it. After all, nature is calling and you have your own bathroom. There's no need for questionable rest stops or gas stations if you have an RV. During the coronavirus lockdown, this was especially important as public bathrooms were shuttered, along with the rest stops and the buildings housing them.

I remember a day in late August 2019 when I was driving in pouring rain along I-90, heading toward my family's home in Massachusetts. I really needed to use the bathroom. No problem. I had my own. I found a very wide turnout, put the van in park, and set the parking brake. I left the engine running while I dashed to the back to do my business. I was just about done when I heard a knock on the side of the sliding door. It almost gave me a heart attack. Before opening the sliding door, I took a peek out the side window. After all, it might be Freddy Krueger out there in the pouring rain. Fortunately for me, it was a highway patrol officer. I opened the door.

"You okay, ma'am?" he asked.

"I'm fine, officer," I replied. "I just needed to pee."

"Excuse me, ma'am?"

"I needed to pee. When you're old and need to pee, you *need* to pee."

"Well, ma'am," the officer said, trying to suppress a chuckle, "the next time you need to pull over to pee, please turn on your hazard lights."

People often ask me if I feel safe when I stay in parking lots. Yes, I do, providing I use common sense and follow my gut. Several of the RVing apps I use will give reviews of places to stay. I read those reviews. I have stayed all by myself in parking lots with no other RVs or trucks around and felt perfectly safe. One time, early on in my journey, I drove into a Walmart parking lot and immediately got bad vibes. My spidey-sense was on alert. I drove around the lot, but the feeling persisted. I left. A few miles down the road, I found a truck stop where I felt quite at ease. Tired or not, I pay attention to my gut. I will pull into a parking lot or other overnight spot, sit in my van and simply observe the activities, vehicles, and people coming and going, before settling in for the night.

A word here about professional long-haul truckers. In some places, RVs park where the big rigs park. Most truck stops and rest areas have separate areas, but not all, especially retail store parking lots. Of course, in a van, I tend to park where cars park, but large RVs and travel trailers often use truck areas. When sharing a parking lot with these professional rigs, I park as far away from them as I can so that they can easily and safely come and go. They are on a tight schedule. The majority of these truckers are also very polite and professional. I have met several in my travels, including a charming young woman. If you need help or road information, they will usually give you guidance. I have had several approach me, curious about my tiny rig. Some of my favorite roadside diners were suggestions from truckers.

Most places that allow overnight parking expect you to patronize their store, if that applies. And you should. You should also be a good neighbor. Some places that used to allow RV parking stopped because of bad behavior from RVers, like leaving trash or making it look like a campground with grills and chairs. I stayed at one Walmart where several RVs joined together and had a party. WRONG! You are OVERNIGHTING only. For FREE. Keeping a low, tidy profile will protect the practice for everyone.

I will specifically look for a Walmart when I need supplies like groceries. Free is not really free, but you can always use something. Many Walmarts also have hair salons, and I will get my hair cut when I need it. If I stay in a restaurant or casino parking lot, I will go in and have a meal.

You should also ask permission to stay in these lots, or at least check to make sure they allow it. I admit to being loosey-goosey about this practice. I will not bother if I see other RVs in the lot, but I will if I'm the only one. Many casinos require you to register with security, and some will charge you a small fee, even if you are eating and/or gambling at their establishment. Some enterprising casinos have even installed RV parks with hookups.

Another question I'm asked regarding overnight parking in lots is about the noise. Yes, they can be noisy and, if you are noise sensitive, they might not be for you. After all, people are coming and going, especially if it is a 24-hour type establishment or contains a lot of professional big rigs. I lived for years on a very busy street in Los Angeles, so traffic noise does not bother me one bit. It can even lull me to sleep. A lot of these places are near train tracks. As long as the train isn't running right next to me, I sleep like a baby. One Labor Day weekend, I was camping in a Wisconsin campground on the border with Iowa and the train tracks were so close my van shook every time a train went by. The romance of trains was lost on me that trip.

Besides parking lots and rest areas, I also overnight in campgrounds, although usually I save those for longer stays. My preferences are National Parks and Army Corps of Engineers campgrounds. These are usually quite nice. Plus, I get the campsite for half price because I have a Lifetime National Parks Senior Pass, which I like to call my old fart's pass. Often, National Parks will not have hookups, but are in really beautiful places. After that, my preferences include small city and county parks.

Small-Town America is wonderful, and many communities have their own small RV parks. These became a life-saver during the initial coronavirus shutdown. Usually they allow one to four nights free. Most have electrical hookups and water, and some even offer sewer hookups. Although free, I usually leave a donation if they have a donation box, or I patronize local businesses. Some of these small-town parks charge a small fee, which is generally done on the honor system.

There is also free dispersed camping on Bureau of Land Management (BLM) land, but most of that is in the west. Some of these places can be difficult to get to or off the beaten path, but I have stayed in some that were very convenient. One of my favorites is The Alabama Hills in California. This is an area by Lone Pine with incredible rock formations that has a long history of being used for movies and TV shows. Another favorite is outside of Twenty-Nine Palms, California, just north of Joshua Tree National Park by a solar farm. Just a few miles south of the South Rim of the Grand Canyon are a lot of National Forest roads with great free camping. I stayed on one for a week with a friend while we explored the Grand Canyon.

In early 2020, I spent most of January through March in Quartzsite, Arizona, a mecca for dispersed camping and RVs. Some are free and you can stay up to fourteen days. Others have small fees with longer allowed stays. I learned about most of these places from friends. During those months, my friends and I bounced around from place to place, staying until services started shutting down for the season and because of the coronavirus.

I do stay on occasion in privately owned RV parks, but not often. My home base is the Escapees Rainbow's End RV Park in Livingston, Texas, and it's nice enough, has friendly folks, and is convenient to the town of Livingston.

Plus, I get a discount for being an Escapees member. But as a rule, I avoid privately owned places. They tend to be more expensive and crowded, often with people living full-time or nearly full-time in them. They have their own mini-culture. It's not my thing, but perfect for folks looking for that community feel.

There are memberships you can purchase that allow specialty overnight parking. When I first started, I had a couple. Now, I only belong to one: Harvest Hosts. This is a network of wineries, farms, breweries, museums, and markets that allows you to park on their properties. Again, you are expected to purchase their goods or visit their attractions. My favorites are the farms, markets, and museums.

PREPARE, PREPARE, PREPARE

With still two years before retirement, I got busy getting ready for my new life. I had a calendar countdown app on my phone and was now counting down the days with it. I was obnoxious about it, even showing it to my bosses and co-workers.

Those few years gave me time to prepare properly for life on the road. This is where the checklist I'd already started came in handy. It may sound like overkill to many, but in the end I was prepared and had things in place that made my transition to a nomadic writer much easier. Life on the road can be a shock at first and there will be bumps and bruises, not to mention pandemics. I was reduced to tears by the second week of full-time travel, and that wasn't the only time. Being prepared can help absorb that shock and give you confidence as you rip your stationary life up by its roots.

Things I had to consider or tend to prior to life on the road:

- *New glasses and a spare pair.* I acquired these several months before leaving so that I could get comfortable with the new prescription.
- *Updating my medical and dental checkups.* This also included getting a supply of medications I used.
- *Updating medical insurance.* Since I was retiring and over 65, I researched and signed up for Medicare when the time came, making sure I had a supplement that was portable. This is very important to those using Medicare. Know what your insurance covers before getting on the road.
- *Where to call "home."* I researched states that were more friendly to full-time nomads regarding taxes, insurance, and healthcare. The three most prominent are South Dakota, Texas, and Florida. I chose to become a Texas resident. The state was central and I already had many friends there. I became an official Texas resident, including vehicle registration, driver's license, and voter registration. Before I even left California, I had a Texas address in place and had changed over a lot of my important information and accounts to that address.
- *Mail forwarding.* This is tied in with choosing a domicile. My mailing address is in Texas through Escapees, a company focused on the needs of RVers. They receive my mail and hold it. Every now and then, I call them up and they forward it to wherever I tell them. It works great for me, especially since I get most of my

correspondence online. Their address in Livingston, Texas, is my official address.

- *RV household items.* I got rid of a lot of my belongings and replaced many with more RV-friendly ones. I bought new microfiber towels that dried fast and took up a lot less room than my fluffy towels from home. I also got rid of my dishes and cookware and replaced them with nearly unbreakable Corelle dishes and Magma stackable cookware. Many full-time RVers use paper plates. I decided early on that if the van was going to be my home, then it would be outfitted like a home. I like eating off real dishes and using real utensils. My van utensils are the same ones I used in my apartment. I had to get new sheets and blankets because the van has twin beds and my bed in the apartment was a queen. Those queen sheets were old and needed to be replaced, but I made do, as I made do with a lot of worn-out things at the end, knowing I would soon replace them with RV-friendly items.

- *RV-specific items.* I started a list of things I needed specifically for the RV, such as sewer attachments, camping gear, etc. Over time, I bought these or acquired them. I had a wish list on Amazon and many friends and family bought these and other RV household items for me as birthday, Christmas, and retirement gifts. There was a time when I got excited about gifts of jewelry. Now, the gift of a sewer attachment could send me into a titter.

- *Downsizing.* Before I could move into *Novella,* I had to downsize everything I owned. I got rid of about ninety percent of my belongings. Clothing, dishes, and other household goods were given to charities or friends and neighbors. Old sheets and towels were given to animal shelters. Cartons and cartons of books were given to the Friends of the Library of my local branch. I had an "apartment" sale and sold a lot of my furniture and other items that way. During the downsizing, I set aside several sections in my apartment. One was for things going into the RV, another for things being given to family and friends, and lastly one for items definitely for sale. I digitized photos I wanted to keep from albums. Near the end, after I had *Novella* and needed to get out of the apartment quickly, I also hired people to help me clean out cupboards and closets. It was good money well spent since I was still working full-time and was now exhausted from juggling it all.

Honestly, as excited as I was about embarking on my new life, I was also shocked and upset watching people pick over and comment on my possessions, my memories, and my life's material existence. I had to fight the urge to yell, "Put that down. It's not for sale!"

I had to keep reminding myself that I had to live smaller in order to live larger.

Even now, a few years into my travel, I am still constantly downsizing. About twice a year, I reorganize the van and take stock of what I carry. If something was not worn or used in the past year, there's a good chance it's not going to continue down the road. I lost a lot of weight during my first year on the road. During my third year, I finally got rid of my larger clothing and bought new things. Not more clothing, but replacement clothing.

Also, by the time I bought and moved into *Novella*, I had one cat. My other had passed away a couple of years before. Poor B was over 19 years old and beside herself with all the changes. She also suffered from feline dementia. Yes, that's a thing. I moved her into the van, which she hated immediately. It terrified her, even though I brought her bed, bowls, and a few favorite toys. Whenever I had to drive the van, she nearly had a heart attack and often vomited. After sharing a queen bed with me for almost two decades, she hated sleeping on the van's twin bed and spent many a night walking up and down it—and me—trying to find a suitable spot. She passed away a month after I moved into the van full-time. The vet thought she would be dead long before all this madness began, but she showed us all and lived a year and a half past the vet's prognosis. There was one thing B loved about the van. She loved being able to sit in front of the open sliding door and watch the world come and go through the screen. Two years after being on the road, I adopted another cat. She is a young rescue that a friend of mine was fostering in Minnesota. I named her Moxie. Moxie hates when the van is moving, but when it's not, she loves it. She loves all the windows and seeing different things and new people. She has been a great companion. Like B, she also loves watching everything that goes on in our moveable life.

4

I'VE GOT THIS

After I took possession of *Novella*, downsized my belongings, and got rid of my apartment, it was a waiting game. I lived for nine months in an RV park on the outskirts of Los Angeles. My commute to work was awful now, but I survived with audiobooks and the knowledge that it was for a limited time. I still had my compact car, so *Novella* stayed at the park instead of making that nasty commute, saving wear and tear and gas. I took *Novella* out for long weekends of camping. She was everything I wanted. My first real camping trip was a meet-up with other Travato owners in Yosemite. I'd never been to Yosemite, so it was a double thrill.

During the meet-up, I met a lot of other owners who, until now, I'd only known from the Facebook group. There were a few things I wanted done to *Novella*, and a couple of the men graciously did them for me. I also learned a lot more about my van from these good people. It's amazing how much I can do now myself.

While I continued to wait for my retirement, a couple of things happened in the van requiring repairs. First, a small plastic coupling on the fresh water tank failed. After that, the regulator on the propane tank stopped working.

One of the things I really like about owning a Travato is the TOAW group on Facebook. If members have a question or concern, we can post it and usually someone can help or make suggestions. When I mentioned I had a water leak and where I thought it was located, people commented on it, several suggesting that it was this plastic joint or coupling. I was also informed that I would need to double check it to make sure. A daunting task to a newbie since it was behind one of the beds near the floor, but at least I wasn't on the road trying to do this. After taking everything out of the storage area under my bed, I unscrewed the back panel that separated the storage from the water tank. Sure enough, there was the leak, and it was coming from under the coupling. I took photos, then contacted one of the mobile RV repair people recommended by the RV park. He could come the next day. Perfect. Meanwhile, I drained the tank.

By taking apart the panel myself and sending the repair man photos, I saved myself a lot of money by cutting down the time he spent working on it. When he showed up, he had a coupling he believed would fit. It did. He took off the old and replaced it with the new, which was a chore in itself considering its location. He had me put some water in the fresh water tank and we waited to see if the leak was fixed. It was. He asked if I needed him to replace the panel. "No thanks, I can do it myself," I told him proudly. I put the panel back on and loaded up the storage area. To this day, the repair has held.

I called the same repair man when my propane regulator conked out. Again, using help from the online group, I ordered the part ahead of time. All the repair man had to do was change out the old one. Another item that has held the repair.

While I waited to go on the road, I made a lot of small modifications to my van to make it more comfortable for traveling and living. The prior owner had already made many of the modifications I wanted. These included installing a privacy curtain between the coach and cab areas, a wraparound shower curtain track, dividers in one of the galley drawers for utensils, and hooks on the back outside wall for hanging hoses and other maintenance tools. Over time, I have made other little fixes or adopted suggestions from other Travato owners, such as a small shelf above my bed, a storage shelf and basket above my sliding door, converting my hanging closet to a drawer system, and installing shoe racks. Every time someone posts a modification in the TOAW group, I check to see if it would make my life in the van easier.

The largest thing I have ever done on my own was install an access door to the plumbing and heating system under the bed on the driver's side of my van. There is a hatch, but it is on the side in the narrow aisle. To get at problems or even to change the water filter, I would have to lie belly down on the floor. Not happening. Several of the other owners had cut a hatch in the bed platform above, making it easier to access this important part of the van. Long story short, I borrowed a friend's jigsaw and got to work. Following the instructions of another Travato owner, I cut a hole in the bed platform above the heating and water systems and installed a marine-type frame and door. Not a single drop of blood was shed.

I have never considered myself a mechanical person, but since owning this marvelous machine, I've become quite adept at using minor tools and coming up with my own modifications and fixes. I have replaced headlamp bulbs, both cabin and engine air filters, and unclogged the toilet. YouTube is your friend. You can learn how to do most anything on YouTube. All it takes is common sense and putting aside the fear of failure.

Okay, so now I would like to make a public service announcement. It involves mansplaining, although I've known women with this bad habit, too. But mostly, it comes from men. I wasn't on the road long when I encountered men who, in their desire to help, were condescending and often downright rude. They assumed I didn't have a clue simply based on my gender, and possibly my age. At first, I just gritted my teeth, but not long into my journey I started standing my ground.

About a month after I took to the road, I backed into a campsite at an RV park when an elderly man in a very old and fairly dilapidated trailer in the next space came out and started telling me everything I was doing wrong. He told me I needed to back up more to reach the sewer connection and water, even though I was fine. He told me I should have gotten a trailer instead of a van. He yammered on and on about my rig's shortcomings. Seriously. I hadn't even turned off the engine yet. Then, he said he would hook up my water and sewer for me, even though I had not backed up as he had initially instructed. I thanked him but stated I could do it myself. He insisted. I insisted I didn't need his help, but thank you very much. I explained that I only hooked up when I needed to dump my waste tanks or fill my fresh water tank, a practice I continue to follow years later. He advised me that was the incorrect way to RV. When he opened my sewer hose storage door on the side of *my* van and started to remove the hose, my patience went down the sewer drain. I stuck my head out the window and shouted,

"Leave my shit alone!" Of course, by saying *shit* I meant my sewer hose, but it could have also been taken literally in this situation. He put it back, backed off, and barely spoke to me during the remainder of my stay. Which was just fine with me.

I once had a man take my water hose out of my hand when I was getting ready to fill my fresh water tank. Then, he tried to attach it incorrectly to my van in his quest to *help*. "Um, it does not go on the black tank flush," I explained, only to be told that my system was set up wrong. *Yeah. Right.* If I hadn't insisted he back away and let me take care of it myself, he would have flooded my black tank.

Before you label me a crabby old bitch, let me say that I do like it when people offer to help. See, that's the difference. *Offer.* Several times, men have approached and asked if I needed help. If I do, I smile, say thank you, and tell them what I need. I've been offered—and gratefully accepted— help with things like being directed while backing into a particularly long and twisty drive at a campsite, and getting my sewer hose unstuck from the hook up. If I don't need help, I will thank them for the offer. I am also not adverse to asking for help when I need it.

On the other hand, I was at a dual dump station once and nearly done with my waste tank dumping when I noticed the man at the dump next to me having a tough time hooking up his hose to his travel trailer. I asked him if he would like some help with it. He looked me up and down and was clearly appalled that a woman, an elderly woman no less, thought he needed help. Curtly, he told me no. He was still fiddling with his dump hose as I drove off. A similar thing happened at a campground when I was next to several college-age men camping in a rental RV. They were having a tough time figuring out how to hook up the sewer connection. I asked them if they would like some help with it. Again, they appeared insulted at my offer and assured me the rental place had shown them a video on how to do it. Okey dokey. I sat in my camp chair and hoped that if they did have an accident of the poop kind, it didn't flow into my campsite.

For some unknown reason, my rig burns out headlamp bulbs quickly. I have become quite adept at changing them. At a large meet-up, someone needed help getting his headlight bulb changed. His wife came to me to borrow some tools I use for it and I gladly offered my help. She accepted. However, her husband, while he was happy to use my tools, refused my help, saying he would wait for one of the men to come over and help him. Fine by me. While he did that, I joined some friends for a cocktail. By the way, I now have LED headlight bulbs and haven't needed to change them since they were installed.

My all-time favorite gender snub happened even before I owned my van. I was talking with a dealer and asking questions about the model I wanted. After a few questions, the salesman cut me off and told me to have my husband come by to talk with him. Seriously?

There are a lot of women who travel in RVs. Many of them travel alone, as I do. In my experience, I have noted far more solo female travelers than solo men out and about. Many of these women are older. Trust me, we are far from incompetent.

So, what's the takeaway here? Male or female, ask someone if they need help before you assume they are inept.

5
_____

OH POOP

If there's one thing people have always asked me about, before and after I got the van, it's how I handle emptying the black and gray tanks. For those not in the know, the black tank is the sewer tank and the gray tank is the dirty water from the sink and shower. No one seemed to think it was something I could or would ever do. Mention an RV's black tank and everyone pictures the disastrous scene in the Robin Williams movie *RV* where waste explodes everywhere.

I am not a hot house flower. Emptying the black and gray tanks was something I knew I would have to do. It's simply a fact of life when traveling in an RV. Even if you have a composting or a cassette toilet, you still have to deal with getting rid of your waste. Before I picked up the van, I had viewed many YouTube videos showing how to empty waste tanks, and felt confident in my ability to do it.

In the TOAW group, I am known for a couple of things. Two of them involve poop stories. My own Robin Williams mishaps, thankfully, were not nearly as disastrous, but it was pretty disgusting.

The second full day I owned my van, I planned on stopping in Texas on my way back to California to meet my friend, Jeanne, and some of her librarian friends for dinner. They were considering inviting me to speak at a few of their libraries. No problem. I was making good time on the road and would be there in plenty of time for dinner.

Enter a calamity of the poop variety.

Around noon that day, I decided to pull into a rest stop with the intention of taking a shower in the van and putting on clean clothes. When I arrived at Jeanne's house, I would be ready for dinner. Unfortunately, I discovered that I had not turned off my water pump or thoroughly turned off the water in my bathroom sink, which flows into the black tank in my particular model, unlike the galley sink, which flows into the gray tank. While I was blissfully driving, the running water had filled the black tank, causing it to back up into the toilet and spill into the shower pan. Oh yeah, I had a shower full of shit. Fortunately for me, I had only been using the van for a couple of days, but it was still pretty revolting.

I immediately turned off my water pump and faucet. While I surveyed the mess, I sat on my bed and started to laugh. I was still hysterically cackling when my phone rang. It was Ron, the man who had sold me the van, checking up on me. He asked if I was laughing or crying. When I told him what had happened, we laughed together. It was the kind of laughing that brings on hiccups and makes you pee a little. He asked what I was going to do. Clean it up, of course, I told him. Next, I called Jeanne to let her know I would be late.

I did make it to Jeanne's and we did go to dinner, but it was much later and all but one of her friends had bailed. By the time I arrived, I was exhausted. The first thing I did after I got off the phone with Ron was drive to a truck stop with a dump station and empty both tanks and refill my fresh water tank. I also went to the local Walmart and bought a couple pairs of heavy rubber gloves and disinfectant cleaner. I always carry gloves for dumping my tanks, but this called for heavier gloves. I drove back to the rest stop and spent the afternoon scrubbing the entire bathroom, every nook and cranny. When I was done, I put on a clean pair of gloves, got a clean cloth, and scrubbed it again until I was satisfied it was clean. Needless to say, I have never traveled with the water pump on since, and I have installed a turnoff valve on the end of the faucet as a safeguard.

Several people in the TOAW group have told me that when they learned of that mishap and how I handled it, they knew I could handle pretty much anything on the road.

The next situation involved toilet clogs. When I got back to California and was ensconced in an RV park full-time until my retirement, I had a bad toilet clog. Nothing I did cleared it. Fortunately, I could use the RV park's restroom during this setback. Finally, I donned rubber gloves and stuck my hand down the toilet pipe. Yeah, *ewww*, I know. But it had to be done. I became known as the owner who put her arm down the toilet pipe. I cleared it, but it happened again. After the third time, I called a mobile repair man.

The repair man immediately unclogged the pipe using a wand that hooks to a water hose. He also gave my black tank a good flushing and advised not to dispose of toilet paper in the toilet since it seemed it was catching on something before it dropped into the holding tank. I bought the same tool he used, just in case of future problems. I have not tossed toilet paper down there since, nor have my hand and arm had to revisit the place where no one wants to go. But my reputation sticks.

If talking about this makes you uncomfortable, then you are not a true RVer. RVers tend to talk about waste and black tank issues and equipment quite frequently. It's part of our life. We don't use the bathroom and flush, not giving a thought to where the waste is going. An RV is basically an outhouse on wheels, and if you own one, you had better not be squeamish about it.

6

WEATHER, IT'S A THING

When I lived in Southern California, which was for most of my life, I never gave weather much thought. Weather in that area of the country is pretty even keel most of the time. The rare times big rainstorms came roaring through, flooding and causing mudslides, you paid attention. Even city streets and low intersections could flood. When I lived in other parts of the country, I only paid attention to the immediate weather forecasts and dressed and behaved accordingly.

Weather on the road is a whole different thing. You follow it not just daily, but throughout the day, and for several days into the future. I have a couple of weather apps on my phone, including one with radar and notification capabilities. I track not only the weather of the area I'm in, but the weather where I'm going in the next week or two. I often need to make decisions on travel plans based on weather, and change direction if needed. I learned this on my first day on the road when I found myself, dressed in capris and a T-shirt, driving through a freak snowstorm on my way to Anza-Borrego Desert State Park.

At first, it was just flurries. Then, it got heavier and heavier. At times, you couldn't tell the sky from the ground. I wasn't sure what to do. Should I pull over somewhere and wait it out? Keep going? I was worried about pulling over because, with the snow cover, I couldn't tell if the shoulder was flat or a shallow ditch. I kept going, keeping my van in the tracks left by the cars ahead, going slow, and watching their tail lights.

Several white-knuckled miles later, I saw cars stuck along the side, and several tow trucks. I kept going. The snow continued. It was dark now. Several miles later, the snow was melting before it hit the road. The road was wide and clear . The road to the campground was curvy but also clear, with nice bright lane dividers. I was ecstatic to see the campground office. The ranger was so nice. He told me it was a freak snowstorm that caught everyone by surprise. I tucked the van into my campsite, turned on the heat, and sat down with a nice glass of wine. A trip that was supposed to take about three and a half hours took over five.

My first day as a nomad, I got a good education on watching weather, but I still wasn't an A student.

A few months later, I was staying in Tyler State Park in Texas when the temperatures took a late-season nosedive. It dropped into the mid 20s overnight and my van was not winterized. I became quite worried. My first full day there got above freezing, but barely. This is very hard on the van's pipes if not winterized. I made it through the night by running my heat on high. Fortunately, I was plugged into electricity, also known as being on shore power, and not using up all my propane. Several times in the night, I woke up hot because of the heat, but I needed to keep the van super warm. Most of my plumbing is inside the van under the bed on the driver's side and near the heating unit. The issue becomes serious when the freezing temperatures go on for a few days without ever going above freezing. The next day, temperatures rose to the upper 40s, which was great for my pipes. One thing did freeze, though. The pipe from the toilet to the black tank is slightly curved. It didn't break, but I noticed it wasn't draining properly. When it was only twenty-nine degrees outside, I took the flexible tool for toilet clogs and pushed it down the toilet, plunging up and down until the ice broke and the toilet bowl was able to drain properly. While I was doing that, a couple all bundled up against the cold strolled by and asked if I needed help. It was just about that time when I heard the satisfying crack of breaking ice in the pipe. I thanked them but said my mission was accomplished. What a glamorous lifestyle!

Just over a week later, I got schooled in weather in a big way.

I was about forty to fifty miles from Roswell, New Mexico, when I drove through the most awful storm I had been in yet. The storm hit hard and fast. It poured rain and flooded the road in just minutes. Hail pelted down from a dark sky. Hail is one of my biggest weather fears. I kept looking for a place with cover, but I found none to accommodate the size of my van. My windshield and the van got through it unscathed, as did my solar panels. I pulled over and looked at one of my apps and saw that there was a Walmart three miles away. I crawled through the rain those few miles, often going through intersections with deep water. By the time I got to Walmart, my nerves were shot. There were already several RVs taking shelter there. The rain stopped and the sun came out briefly, but trouble was far from over. Next came the wind, blowing and gusting and rocking my van with vigor.

I had a weather app, but none with radar at that time. I

quickly downloaded one and tracked the storm. There was a tornado warning for my area. In fact, there were tornado watches all over. The news was calling this cyclone bomb weather and particularly warned high-profile vehicles to stay off the road. At just shy of ten feet tall, my van is considered a high-profile vehicle.

The second day, the wind continued to batter the van back and forth. I even pointed her nose into it to help lessen the movement. I never left the van. I couldn't have opened the doors if I'd wanted to. The wind roared and blew at 50+ miles per hour. Sometimes, it was close to 70 miles per hour. All that day, it felt like a very long plane trip with head-thumping turbulence. I even battled motion sickness. The van rocked, bounced, shook, and shivered all day. At times, I even feared for my life.

Since the situation in New Mexico, I have been in a couple of other big windstorms. They still terrify me. I keep a close eye on my weather apps and try to plan travel accordingly. If I can, I go around the bad weather. If I cannot, I find a fairly safe place and sit still, waiting it out.

A few years into living on the road, I found myself being ousted from a campground in Mississippi because of flooding. I'd been pretty ill the night before and was planning on spending the day in bed when I got a knock on my van's sliding door. My visitor was a young ranger. He told me I had a couple of hours to vacate the campground because the lake it was on was expected to breach its banks with the storm coming in that night. They'd had several recent rainstorms and I'd noticed that the water was slowly creeping into the campground around the edges. That night, they were expecting a big storm. Sick or not, I had to quickly dress and get out of there. I was refunded for the remaining days of my stay, but on the fly, I had to find someplace to safely land. I ended up driving over three hours to another campground that was out of the storm's reach.

Another time, I had to take refuge in the concrete building of a visitors' center at a rest area because of a tornado. I had pulled into the rest area to wait out the bad weather. Shortly after, the weather alert on my phone went off, scaring me to death. Then, I heard the local tornado siren. I was traveling with a cat by then. I packed her up in her carrier, grabbed my laptop and purse, and ran in pouring rain and heavy wind the short distance to the visitors' center. There, I hunkered down with about a dozen other people. A tornado had touched down less than five miles away.

I believe in caution when traveling in bad weather. Sometimes, I find myself in rain hard enough to obscure the road. When this happens, I find a rest area or a parking lot, pull in, and wait it out. I do the same with wind and fog. A few minutes or hours off the road can mean protecting my life.

7

YOU ARE SO BRAVE

Don't you get lonely?
   Aren't you afraid?
   You are so brave.

These are a few of the questions and comments I get regularly about traveling alone.

Yes. Sometimes, I get lonely. But not often. I prefer to travel alone. Other singles may prefer to travel in groups or caravans, or with a couple of friends. I like the freedom traveling alone gives me. If I want to change plans on a whim, there is no one to consult and no compromises to be made.

Loneliness is not about being alone. You can be lonely in a crowd or even in a relationship. Being alone on the road is often full and satisfying. You really get to learn a lot about yourself as you travel miles of road and stop to see amazing things. If I do find myself hankering for company, I can always reach out via the Internet or phone to my friends and family.

Getting to know yourself means facing new situations and seeing how you fare. How do you react in stressful situations? How well do you problem solve? I learned that I am much more capable mechanically than I expected. Before living on the road in an RV, if I needed something done, I called and paid someone to do it. Since moving into my van, I have learned that I can do most anything I put my mind to, with some limitations, of course. Being a rather rotund older woman, I have no interest in crawling under my van. The last thing I need is to get stuck. The very idea of that makes me want to hyperventilate. It's also not a pretty sight watching me get up off the ground with my often-gimpy knees. I also won't climb a ladder.

Spending so much time alone means you must be or become comfortable in your own skin and with silence. Some people can't tolerate being alone for hours on end. I thrive on it. Maybe that's why being a writer is the perfect career for me. Even when I travel with other RVers, I often spend much of the morning alone in my van writing. Don't get me wrong, I like people, and I like spending time with people. I'm not tongue-tied in front of three hundred people or three people. I am an extroverted introvert. Sometimes, when I am around a lot of people, I feel drained or oversaturated, especially if I'm giving a speech or doing a book event. Even before I began living in a van, I would often hole up in my apartment for entire weekends to recharge.

I meet a lot of people traveling alone like myself. Most seem to be happy and comfortable in their solitude. We eat alone. Sightsee alone. Sleep in parking lots alone. As a kid, I spent a lot of time on my own. My parents worked a lot and were often too absorbed in their unhappy marriage to spend much time with me. I spent hours in my room with my nose in a book. Such a childhood better prepared me for my life as a single nomad.

In spite of the above, I love meeting people on the road and traveling or camping with them from time to time. I often go to meet-ups with other van owners. If I'm not working, I'm delighted when people stop by my campsite to chat. People are interesting and fun, and we can learn so much from each other. You can be a loner and still be sociable.

One thing I've noticed in my travels is how many women aged sixty and up are traveling solo in RVs of one kind or another. I love talking to women like me and learning about them and why they chose this lifestyle. I know why I did it, but why did they? This is not scientific research, by any means, but by my guesstimate and experience, there are many more single older women living on the road than single older men. The reasons vary. Some lost their homes, partners, jobs, and support, and are trying to exist by living in a vehicle. But most of the women who travel alone that I know or have met in my travels are not doing it for this reason. For centuries, women have been boxed into conformity and have had expectations foisted on them. Most of the female solo travelers I have met have been married and raised families. Some are widowed, some divorced. Some, like me, have never married. Most have had careers. Now that they are older, they are enjoying freedom from these obligations and traveling in search of themselves and a world outside of their comfort zone. Many have told me that their families are not happy with their choice to travel, especially alone, yet they struck out on a new path for their later years. Maybe we're brave for stepping outside of expected conformity.

Most of the time that I was in Arizona in early 2020, I traveled with a loose group of other Travato owners. Sometimes, there would be two of us, other times six. People came and went at our different locations. I bonded with another Travato owner named Stacy and we traveled together much of that time. Both being loners and people who work from our vans, we understood the need to get our work done and to also give others space. Over the years, we have traveled quite a bit together, always successfully. While I was finishing this book, Stacy and I were on the road together for several months visiting the Canadian Maritime provinces and the northern United States. Yet, as much as we enjoy each other's company, we're always ready to part ways and go solo again.

I also get asked about romance on the road. I always thought it would be perfect for my lifestyle to meet a nice, interesting man who traveled full-time or often in his RV. We could meet-up from time to time for companionship, spend days or weeks together, but not be bound together full-time. In my first year, I met a couple of men who were interested in me. One I liked a lot, but not enough to form a relationship, not even a casual one. During the early months of the pandemic shutdown, I met another man. He was a full-time RVer who was doing the same thing I was, sheltering in place in his RV, moving from one small city park to another in a circuit. We kept running into each other here and there, getting to know each other better each time. We finally evolved from being friends to a casual couple. The last few weeks I spent in Texas before states started opening up, we traveled together. In time, he also left Texas and we met up in North Dakota. But again, as much as I enjoy this fun, intelligent man's company, I would become eager to be off by myself. And that had nothing to do with him.

The second part of the loneliness question is about safety. People always ask if I feel safe traveling alone. I do. That is usually followed by the comment, "You are so brave."

Whether you are a man or a woman, you must be aware of your surroundings, be it people, wildlife, weather, or geography. Being aware will help you avoid getting into a sticky situation, or help you get out of one. Bravery has nothing to do with it. I do not feel *brave* to be doing this alone. I feel confident and aware.

As I mentioned earlier, there have been times when I've rolled into a parking lot to spend the night and my spidey-sense goes on alert, buzzing like an annoyed hornet. I always listen to it. When this happens, I don't spend the night there and look for another place where my internal sensors hum peacefully.

Safety is another reason why I didn't choose a travel trailer for this journey. I wanted to be in a one-piece, self-contained vehicle. The type of RV where, if the need arose, I could simply hop out of bed, step into the cab, and drive off. Often, I dry camp, meaning without hookups, but even if I'm in a spot with hookups, I'll only connect the power cord. It makes a needed get-away much faster and easier. I only hook up to water and sewer when I need to refill my water tank or dump my waste tanks.

Safety issues don't just mean stranger danger. I've known RVers who have had to evacuate their campsites because of fires and floods. As noted earlier, I once had to evacuate a campground because of flooding. Being less connected can mean a faster evacuation.

As for weapons and other defense mechanisms, that's a personal choice for each traveler. Just remember, what is legal in one state may not be in the next. Know the laws where you're traveling if you decide to travel with lethal weapons. I believe all RVers should carry some sort of deterrent, even if they are not firearms.

Traveling alone, especially along some of our nation's more rural routes, can also be a bit mind numbing. Couples can chat with each other, but when you're alone, you need to keep alert or be aware of your level of alertness. I've found that listening to audiobooks is a great way to spend hours driving a desert road or maneuvering miles and miles of cornfields. I also listen to news, podcasts, and music. When I find myself getting tired or foggy-minded, I'll get off the road for a little bit. I don't push it when I'm tired, just like I don't push through really bad weather. I prefer rest areas for these short stops, but sometimes a parking lot of a large mall or big box store will do. Once stopped, I'll go outside, stretch, and walk around. If the weather is not great, I'll do stretches in the van. Sometimes, I'll even take a short nap. Whatever it takes to be safe on the road.

8

LET'S TALK MONEY

I get that people don't like to talk about money, but it's very important to have a budget when living as a nomad. Or, at least an outline of one. I admit that I'm not the best at budgeting or handling money, but long before I went on the road I had a working understanding of the costs involved. The big-ticket items would be gas, camping fees, insurance, and food. Plus, I would have to budget for van maintenance and my monthly van payment.

I started following some full-time RVers online, especially those who were transparent about their monthly costs. A couple of them warned against first-year *nutsies* (my word, not theirs), whereby newbies on the road act like they are on vacation and spend more than they should. In the excitement of launching into a new lifestyle, especially one that takes you to a lot of touristy locations, it's easy to forget that you are NOT on vacation. This is your life now and you must act accordingly. It was noted that many full-time newbies end up getting off the road after a year or so because of money issues.

About six months before I bought my van, I took one

last hurrah of a vacation. I went to Hawaii, stayed at one of the top hotels on Waikiki, and even rented a private beach cabana for a couple of days. It was wonderful and I had budgeted for the extravagance. Of course, I was also still employed and not living on retirement income as I am now. But once on the road, I had to remember that the van was my home, not a vacation spot.

I confess that while my first year on the road was not a free-for-all, I didn't listen to the wise words of those who went before me and did spend a lot of money on things that I later kept better watch over. I ate out often and camped at more expensive places than I do now. I went to a lot of meet-ups, zigzagging across the country, which added to my camping and gas expenses. I also had to buy two new tires and have some other van maintenance done. I quickly ran through a lot of cash before I hit the brakes on my expenses.

The breakdown below is a loose outline of my current budget:

Gas — About $600 a month. Sometimes, it is a little more or a little less, depending on gas prices and how much I drive in a month. You might think this seems low, but remember, I travel in a Class B, a camper van that averages 15-16 miles per gallon. On open roads, I can sometimes get 17 miles per gallon. In congested areas, it may drop to 14 miles per gallon. That's a far cry from the RVs that get 8 miles per gallon or even less. Plus, I don't travel every day. When gas prices started going sky high in 2022, I stayed longer in places to save gas money. When the prices lowered, I started traveling more. During the period of the price surge, I had a few months where my monthly gas expense hit $700-$800.

Camping — About $400 per month, and often less. With many RV parks and campgrounds costing around

$60-$70 a night (some in touristy locations even $100+ a night), this might also seem low, but I stay away from RV "resorts" and big RV parks. As stated previously, I prefer Corps of Engineers campgrounds or National Parks where I can use my Lifetime Senior Pass and camp for half off. State parks can be either a bargain or expensive, as some offer special passes or deals to seniors and others add on extra expenses for out-of-state guests. The lowest amount I've ever paid for camping in a month was $8. Yes, you read that right. And it was not when I was parked in my family's driveway or off the road. That month, I mostly dry camped except for one night at a National Park, which was $8. The most I have spent on camping in a month was just over $600. That $600 amount happened in my first year, during which I was staying in more expensive places and not doing as much dry camping.

Another thing to consider is that gas and camping expenses tend to go hand in hand. If I'm scooting all over the country, I can spend around $80 a day for gas, but maybe no money on camping if I'm dry camping each night. But if I stay in one of my favorite campgrounds for a week or so at the average price of $12 per night with my Senior Pass, I can save quite a bit in gas money. It is all about the math.

At the beginning of my fourth year, friends and I discovered a small RV park in Yuma, Arizona. The daily rate was $25, but only $260 (plus electricity) for a month. I had a lot of writing and projects to catch up on, so I decided to stay for a month. Not only did I get a lot of work done, but I saved a lot of money on gas. At the end of my fourth year, I spent much of the winter going between campgrounds rather than traveling all over. One reason was to save money, but my propane was also on the fritz, so I needed to be plugged in for heat. Those months saved me a lot in gas money, even though I paid more in camping fees. By the way, I was without propane for eight months. It took me that long to find someone to fix it, and the repair was around $900.

I also roll my Harvest Hosts stays into my camping budget. Staying at a Harvest Hosts location may be free, but you are expected to patronize their services, whether it be a restaurant, museum, or winery. So, it's really not free. Nice, but not free. When choosing a Harvest Hosts location, I tend to stay only at places where I can use their services or goods, generally restaurants, farms, or an interesting museum. Even the dry camping at a Walmart is not "free." If you do stay in a Walmart parking lot, you are expected to shop at their store. But this is easy, and I put it into my food budget since I buy groceries there. Or sometimes I'll buy gas if they have a station attached, or even get my hair cut if they have a salon.

Food — $300 a month. This is a budget item I'm rather loosey-goosey about. The amount listed is for van food, which is food I prepare and eat at home in my van. It also includes pet food. I love to eat out, but eating out even once a day can add up. I ate out a lot more in my early days, but now I try to keep it down to only a few times a week, and usually just an inexpensive breakfast or lunch. Preparing and eating food in the van is much more cost effective, and it's healthier. I find that I eat out much more when traveling with friends, and I make adjustments for that.

Insurance — Currently, my RV insurance runs about $200 a month for a policy covering full-time RVing. Most policies for full-time RVers are a combination of vehicle and home coverage. Remember, vehicle insurance can vary greatly depending on where you live or are domiciled.

What I pay may be less or more than what you'll be quoted. It also depends if you use your RV for recreation only or full-time living. Plus, not all insurance companies will cover RVs used for full-time living. RV insurance coverage requires research with your personal needs in mind. Health insurance and prescription supplements to my Medicare are about $235 a month.

Phone — This is an expense that depends on the individual user. I have unlimited data on my iPad and iPhone that runs about $130 a month. I get decent coverage in most places for my work. People who work technical jobs on the road may need a more robust communication set up and more costly equipment.

Entertainment — I budget about $150 a month for attractions and entertainment. Some months, I spend very little on this. This includes things like tours, museums, and souvenirs, even the occasional casino visit. It also includes set monthly subscriptions to things like Netflix and other live streaming. I don't spend a lot on souvenirs. First of all, I have no room for bric-a-brac. If I do buy a souvenir, it's either the occasional T-shirt or lapel pin. Mostly, I purchase collectible lapel pins, fastening them on the headliner of the van over the cab section. They take up no room and are relatively inexpensive. They are also fun to look at and remember the places I've been.

Miscellaneous — There are a lot of little expenses in life on the road. Propane is reasonable and is usually only about $20 a month, often less. Unless it's cold at night when I'm dry camping, I only use it for cooking and heating hot water. Laundry is usually about $15 a month. I maintain websites that are billed monthly. There are also small unexpected costs that can arise like parking, etc., plus periodic expenses such as oil changes and pet care.

Emergencies — I try to set aside money each month for emergencies and always have a little cash stash on hand. It's surprising how many businesses I've encountered in rural areas that don't take credit cards, so I always carry some cash. I also have an emergency credit card and another I use only for gas. I got the gas card after my debit card was hacked twice while pumping gas. In addition to being more secure, I can track my monthly gas use easily.

Annual Expenses — I belong to a few RV clubs that bill annually, like Escapees and Harvest Hosts. Plus, my mail service through Escapees is billed annually. There are many RV clubs to join. I started out with a few others and after the first year pared it down to just a couple that I use consistently.

Life on the road can be less expensive than life in a stationary home, but only if you use your head. Otherwise, it can be just as expensive.

9

WORD WARRIOR

Many people I meet tell me I have their dream job. Being a nomadic writer sounds cool and glamorous, doesn't it? A bit romantic, maybe?

One of the main purposes of The Novel RV, which is my brand and my home, is so I can write full-time while I travel. Writing is not my hobby. It is my business. I work at it almost every day. I treat it as a business. It pays me as a business. I am a professional writer.

The Novel RV became my brand on the road. I wanted something other than just my name to promote my books and my new lifestyle. It turned out to be a great decision on my part. I came up with the name before I even bought the van. I had a professional logo created. Before I started traveling, I ordered magnetic signs to affix to both sides near the back. The signs contained the name, logo, and website information. They were one of the best marketing tools I had. As I drove down the road or camped, people took notice of the sign, and even took a photo of it. They looked it up and often contacted me, letting me know they spotted me. Often, they bought my books because of it. I even had readers and friends see the van in parking lots and track me down inside a store or restaurant, or wait for me to return to the van to say hello. Readers wanted their photos taken with *Novella* and the sign. Once, a writer I know spotted the van in a parking lot in Lake Havasu, Arizona. She found me in Denny's having breakfast. We spent the next three hours catching up. Those simple signs connected me to new readers and old friends.

Sadly, at the time of writing this book, I no longer have the signs on my van. When the country became so divided, I started getting not-so-nice remarks from people who looked me up online. So, in the interest of security and my safety, I removed them in late 2020 and have never replaced them.

People follow my journey as The Novel RV on Facebook, Instagram, and even on Patreon, where I maintain a daily journal of my activities, even the really mundane things. People seem fascinated by this type of journey, including the details. For over five years, I have written daily in The Novel RV Journal on Patreon, and it's still going strong. Many of my patrons follow me because I take them places they may never see. Doing that makes me feel like I'm doing something good and useful. I also started a YouTube channel where I post a video on various subjects on nomadic life and writing on occasional Tuesdays, which I call Suesdays.

When I first started my journal on Patreon, I received a lot of flack, even from some other writers. Access to The Novel RV Journal is by subscription only. It's not an expensive subscription, but people still balked. I was determined to stay my course on this matter. I am a professional writer and should be paid for my work. I put a lot of effort and time into my journal posts, including very personal feelings and activities, research, and photos. I'm not sure why a lot of people think writing should be free. People seem to think those of us who create for a living, whether it be writing, music, or art, should make it free to the public. They would never expect a baker to give them a free birthday cake, or a barber to provide a free haircut, or a car mechanic to provide a free transmission service. But when it comes to artistic endeavors, many expect free. The Novel RV Journal was started a few months before I took to the road and it continues to go strong with a nice group of loyal readers. It also provides me with additional income, which I earmark mostly for writing purposes, such as cover artwork and editing, or sometimes unexpected van repairs.

As much fun as it is, writing is a business, and my occupation. I never forget that. Writers write. Period.

Most days, I write two to four hours a day. I don't have set days off. I take a day off when I feel I need it. When I lived in an apartment, I wrote for two hours every morning, Monday through Friday, before going to work. On weekends, I wrote four to six hours a day, more if I was on a tight deadline for a publisher. Once I started traveling, I had to find a new creative rhythm. Over time, I discovered that writing in the late afternoon or early evening suited me best on days I spent driving and sightseeing. I try to be settled somewhere by mid afternoon, which gives me time to write before dinner. I write in Walmart parking lots, rest stops, and truck stops, plus other unusual places. Wherever I rest my head for the night is where I write. That doesn't always work out, but most often it does. On days when I'm camped, I go back to my morning writing schedule. When I camp with friends, I especially like to write in the morning so I can spend time with them later. My writing time is not as rigid as it was when I had a stationary home and a regular job, but almost every day I dedicate part of my time to it.

As I often remind people when they remind me that I'm now retired: I am a retired paralegal, not a retired writer. I may never retire from writing.

By the time I retired from my paralegal career, I had fulfilled all of my publishing contracts, the last one just a year before I started traveling. I decided from that point on that when I wrote more fiction, it would be as an independent author or self-published. I didn't want the stress of deadlines in my new life. Until then, I had been producing two novels a year for two different publishers, plus working a full-time job. The Novel RV became my imprint. I was the writer and publisher, mentored by a few other authors who were doing very well as independents. I wrote what I wanted when I wanted and was happy with that. I wasn't writing at the break-neck pace I was before, and had expanded into travel writing. But life is ever changing, and so are goals. While finishing up this book, I signed with a new publisher for this book, plus three novels. After five years on the road, I felt ready to take on contracts again.

Just after I started traveling, one of my publishers, the one with the rights to most of my books, went out of business. They returned the rights of a few books to me in 2019. In January 2020, they returned the rights to my remaining books. Suddenly, I was faced with a big decision. Should I push forward on the novel I was working on, or put that aside and get these older books reissued and back up for sale? I spoke to a couple of friends and all recommended that I take the time to get my backlist back up for sale, especially since I was finding new readers on the road. To them, these were not old novels, but new-to-them novels.

I was just starting the tedious process of re-editing these

older novels, having new covers created, and republishing them when the COVID pandemic became a serious reality. Travel was becoming difficult. We were all told to stay home. For the first three months of the pandemic restrictions, I used the time to get all of these older novels back up for sale in digital format. I pushed through them, one after the other, until they were done. When I turned my attention back to the novel I had put aside, I didn't have my backlist on my mind.

Through a friend's referral, I was also able to connect with the people who published Winnebago's WinnebaGo-Life blog. This blog features stories about the RV lifestyle, travel, modifications, and advice. I did a few stories for them, then started doing more. I really enjoyed this change of pace from writing fiction. I particularly enjoyed the features I did on other Winnebago owners that involved interviews and getting to know new people. I continue to write for Winnebago once in a while.

While on the road, I also tackled making some of my books available in audio format. I did these myself in partnership with professional narrators/producers on the ACX platform. As with writing a novel, it takes time and there are no shortcuts. Recently, an audiobook publisher started putting out my entire Odelia Grey series in audio. I am so excited about this.

Readers kept asking if I intended to write a series about being on the road. My first non-mystery novel, *Finding Zelda,* puts Zelda Bowen on the road by the end of that book, but the next book in the series, *Zelda Doubles Down*, and subsequent novels in that series, will have her traveling around the country. *Finding Zelda* was originally self-published, but it was the Zelda Bowen series that was picked up by my new publisher. *Finding Zelda* will be reissued under them, followed up with *Zelda Doubles Down* and the third novel in the series.

My creative juices really got fired up when I began a new type of series. I came up with the idea of having a young woman take on a new identity to save her life while living on the road and constantly moving about. Thus, *Dead Woman Driving* was brought to life. Unlike the Zelda Bowen series, it's more of a thriller than a comedy.

As I started envisioning the book, I realized there was too much story to put into one novel, but I wasn't sure it had enough legs for an entire series of novels. Instead of writing traditional novels, I broke the series up into episodes of short story length, publishing a new one periodically. The first few came monthly, but interfered with my other writing, so I started spacing them out to allow for other projects. Serial fiction is nothing new. Many well-known authors have produced serial fiction, such as Charles Dickens and Stephen King. However, when *Dead Woman Driving* was first launched, I did butt up against resistance from many of my usual readers. They wanted a full novel, not pieces of a story. But I persisted, and in time, it caught on. The first few episodes became bestsellers on Amazon in the short fiction category. As more episodes were added, new readers began discovering the series. I have no idea when I will end the *Dead Woman Driving* series, but that is the beauty of a serial novel. It can go on forever, should I choose.

I would like to address reader expectations, which is something writers deal with whether they are nomadic or stationary. Before I became a full-time RVer, I wrote two successful mystery series—the Odelia Grey Mysteries and the Ghost of Granny Apples Mysteries. The Odelia Grey books launched my writing career. I also wrote a short-lived vampire mystery series called the Madison Rose Vampire

Mysteries. I loved writing these books, but they represent twenty-three books written over a relatively short time period. When their contracts were up, I decided to take a break from them. Readers continue to ask for more books in these three series, which warms my heart like you would not believe. But the reality is, authors often need to stretch their creative muscles or they become lazy and redundant. Even some of the most popular authors start new series or do standalone novels as a way to grow and develop their craft. Branching out into the Zelda Bowen books and the *Dead Woman Driving* series helped me to revitalize my creativity. I have written a couple of Ghost of Granny Apples short fiction pieces since being on the road, and will continue writing more of those. I would like to do another Odelia Grey novel, but I'm not sure when that will happen. Or maybe I'll bring Odelia back with short fiction. Right now, my priorities are the new novels under contract. I hope my readers will understand and give my new work a chance.

If you're thinking about writing on the road, remember this: It may sound romantic, but it's no different than writing while sitting in a stationary sticks-and-bricks location. You still have to be committed to your craft, both in time and in continuing to improve it. It's still a business, even if your office is a campground on a lake with the occasional deer or squirrel roaming through.

10

SPEED BUMPS

Shit happens. No matter how much you plan, unexpected stuff has a habit of popping up. I had to buy two new tires during my first month on the road. My propane failed and had to be fixed while on the road. Just as with living in a sticks-and-bricks home, stuff happens to a home on wheels. Be prepared to be thrown an unexpected monkey wrench every now and then.

Sometimes speed bumps come in the form of health issues. By the end of my first month, I found myself battling a bad cold and bronchitis. I stayed in a campground a few extra days during the worst of it and took care of myself. That cost me extra money. In my ninth month on the road, I got a horrible sinus infection. I went to a local clinic, where they examined me and wrote me a prescription for antibiotics.

Sometimes, the health issues are more serious. At the beginning of March 2020, just as the pandemic hit the news but before it became a national shutdown, I started to feel ill. The pain was in my gut and getting worse. I was traveling with another Travato owner to a Travato meet-up in

Agua Caliente in California. We arrived at the meet-up, and that night I knew I needed to get medical care.

The nearest medical facility was an hour away in El Centro, California. I insisted on driving myself there, and my friend insisted on going with me. We left the campground very early in the morning and spent most of the day in the ER, where I was tested for one thing or another. The diagnosis was diverticulitis. On the way back to camp, we stopped at a drugstore and got antibiotic prescriptions filled. It took a few weeks for me to feel one hundred percent again, but I was lucky it wasn't anything more serious, and that I had medical insurance through Medicare. I was also fortunate it happened when it did, since within weeks hospitals would be overrun with COVID patients.

I have had several ER visits during my time on the road. Another diverticulitis attack put me in a small town ER in New Mexico. A swollen toe and joint found me in one in Massachusetts, and then there was the pre-dawn drive to an ER in Texas due to kidney stones. I even had to go to an ER with another full-time RVing friend in Arizona. When traveling and camping, know where the closest medical help is located. You never know when you'll need it.

My general practitioner is in Texas, where I'm domiciled. I make sure I get an annual physical and keep up on my medications and general health. It's very important while being on the road. Make sure your health insurance is portable, meaning usable in most states. I have Medicare with a supplement that covers me most everywhere.

Breakdowns happen. As I write this, my Travato has not had a major breakdown of any kind. There have been things that needed repair, but nothing that kept me sidelined for any period of time. Some full-time RVers are not that fortunate. If you are a full-time RVer and your rig breaks down, you may find yourself living in a hotel while repairs are being done. This costs money, even if you have insurance that covers some of the expense of such a thing. Have a plan in the event you are taken out of commission during this time.

As I've mentioned, have an emergency credit card or cash stash for such unplanned events. Make sure you have a good roadside assistance service. If you break down in the middle of nowhere, the towing bill alone could send you into a swoon if you don't have good service and good insurance.

Then, there are speed bumps that affect everyone and everything. Like a pandemic.

SECTION TWO

THE FIRST YEAR ON THE ROAD (THE HONEYMOON PERIOD)

"Go confidently in the direction of your dreams! Live the life you've imagined."

— Henry David Thoreau

11

NOT THE BEST START TO A NEW LIFE

I call my first year of nomadic life *The Honeymoon Period*. In most marriages, during the first year you have a lot of sex. Then, it starts dropping off. The same goes for full-time nomadic living. During my first year of life on the road, I ran hither and yon around the country. After that, I simmered down and was more aware of my time, miles, and expenses. The excitement is still there, just tempered by better judgment and a desire to enjoy everything more. Now, I want to soak and simmer in my experiences, not splash them on my face and run.

I remember the day I left Los Angeles as clearly as if it were yesterday. It was December 31, 2018. I had been staying in an RV park in Los Angeles for nine months while I got used to living in my van and waited for my retirement date from the law firm where I worked. The day I officially became a nomad, I got up early, took one last long shower in the park's bathhouse, unhooked the van's power, and made sure everything was secure. Then, I sat there. Just sat there in the driver's seat and stared out the window. And I cried. Not long. Not hard. But there were tears.

Holy cow! I'm really doing this!

I was about to drive off into the great unknown. I'd been preparing for this day for a couple of years. Now that the day was here, was I getting cold tires? No, not at all. The tears were not sad tears, but tears of joy mixed with tears of terror. After taking several deep breaths, I mopped up my face, turned on the engine, and drove off toward a new life.

My first day's drive took me from Van Nuys to Anza-Borrego State Park, where I would camp for a few days. As I noted in a previous chapter, I was not too far from my destination when I landed in the middle of a freak snowstorm. I managed to get through it, but my life as a nomadic novelist was not off to the best start. Nor was that the last problem I'd have during my first few weeks. I would definitely be tested by fire.

When I left Anza-Borrego, I headed to Quartzsite, Arizona, to meet up with a bunch of other women who also owned Travatos. I got there with no hitch. On the way to Quartzsite, I passed through miles and miles of desert, including the spectacular Imperial Dunes. The dunes reminded me of pristine mounds of coffee ice cream. Although I'm more of a mountain or beach kind of person, I appreciated the stark and forbidding beauty of the desert. It almost challenges you to love it. I still feel this awe for the desert years later.

From Quartzsite, the other women and I caravanned to Bouse, Arizona, where the Women's Rubber Tramp Rendezvous was being held. This gathering includes women who live on the road in vehicles. The event had classes, seminars, and social events over a few days that preceded the very large Rubber Tramp Rendezvous, the original event started by Bob Wells. Both of those events have changed over the years, but are still major events in the nomad world.

Five of us met up and caravanned over to the event location on BLM land. We were five sleek, expensive, and well-appointed vans traveling along the road through the center of the encampment like parade floats. I felt both exhilarated and uneasy. I was excited for the event. Being new on the road, I had a special high going on in my head. My uneasiness came when noticing some of the other attendees' rigs. Many of these women lived in cars or converted vans and trucks. Many of them were women living on what few resources they had and trying hard to make it work. There were many other nice RVs and trailers there, too, but arriving together, I felt horribly conspicuous, like we were showing off, even though it was not our intention.

I'd never met any of these Travato women in person before, but we all knew each other from the TOAW group on Facebook. Many became good friends. What a hoot. We even had three canines in the mix. When we got to the area where we wanted to camp, we circled the wagons around a stone fire pit a camper before us had built. It was freezing when the sun went down, but the stars were phenomenal.

And here, just a week into my new life, was where I hit speed bump #2.

When I first arrived in Quartzsite, I went to get my propane tank filled. For some reason, the place could not get my tank to take any propane. Propane is my heat source when I'm not plugged into power, and the tank was pretty empty. In the first few years, I had on and off trouble with my propane tank. I did get it filled after leaving Quartzsite, but a few years later, after similar issues, I had to have a major repair done to it. But that was not the second speed bump.

Fast forward to supper time. I left the group to return to my van and fix some dinner. No power. No lights. No generator. No power also meant no water pump, so no water. Nothing. One of my friends came over and suggested I turn on the van engine. She was afraid if it would not work, it would be a real hassle for me to get help. The engine turned over just fine, and in doing so, turned on the lights inside the house part of the van. Also, now the generator worked. This was great news because, with the generator running, I could have dinner and even get some heat and water. But I found out that if I turned off the engine, the generator stopped.

I put out an SOS call to Ron, the man who sold me the van. He had become a friend and since he made so many modifications to the van, I thought he might be able to troubleshoot from afar. Unfortunately, even he was stumped after we tried everything. So, the next morning I left the campground in search of an RV repair place. Being Quartzsite, the RV mecca, I figured it should not be too difficult to find someone to help. And hopefully, not too time consuming or expensive.

Meanwhile, with the help of the generator, I heated up the van as best I could before I went to bed. Wearing flannel pajamas, a sweater, socks, and knit hat, I piled every blanket I had onto the bed. Even with those efforts, it was one of the coldest nights I could ever remember experiencing.

The strange thing is, I should have been upset at this point. After all, I'd been retired all of five minutes, and now this. Everything worked great just that morning. But I wasn't upset. Annoyed as hell, yes. After all, this was not cancer, or nuclear war, or any other horrible thing. It was just a mechanical problem, and those happen to every rig at some time or another. My first scheduled speaking obligation wasn't until mid February in Birmingham, Alabama. If this wasn't fixed and I wasn't on the road long before then, then I would be upset. But for now, I was going to look at this as just an annoyance to be endured and taken care of.

First thing in the morning, I drove away from camp and tried to find help for my system. No one in Quartzsite could or would help. Ron said to come back to California and he would try to troubleshoot it himself. I had picked up the van from Ron's home in South Carolina, but he also lived and worked in Southern California, which was great in this time of crisis. So, just a few days after leaving California, I limped back into the state.

The good news was Ron was able to fix the electrical issue. It was a loose connection involving the coach batteries. They had probably come loose while bouncing over the rough roads of Quartzsite. In no time, I was set to go again. The bad news was, he noted that my front tires were very unevenly worn and suggested I get two new tires and an alignment. I drove around to various nearby tire places, but they either didn't have the tires or didn't have the equipment to mount them on such a heavy vehicle. Finally, I called a Ram dealer in Temecula. They had the tires and could do the work, but not until Monday. It was Friday. I made the appointment and went to the closest campground, which was located at Pechanga Casino in Temecula, to wait.

That was my first casino campground, but not my last. But unlike most of the ones I stay at now, it was not free. I was there three nights waiting to get my tires done. Once the tires were on, I was outta there and ready to restart my journey, which went smoothly from that point.

I have a confession. The day before I got to Ron's, I pulled into a not very nice campground. I still had no power to my coach, but at least it wasn't cold as it had been in Quartzsite. I sat in the dark with a lantern and crappy take-out food and had myself a good cry. We're talking a down-right ugly cry. I recorded this breakdown and posted it on The Novel RV YouTube channel for everyone to see. I may have come momentarily unraveled, but I was optimistic that I could get over these hurdles. After all, this was my dream, and I was not about to shove it aside over a simple battery issue.

The rest of January was spent taking care of moving my domicile to Texas. I landed in Livingston, Texas, at the Escapees RV Park, which became my new address as of the first of the year. Using the RV park as a home base, I took care of getting *Novella* inspected and registered in Texas, got a new driver's license, and registered to vote in the state.

I chose Texas as my new home for several reasons. It's one of the states with favorable tax laws for full-time RVers and retirees. It's also inexpensive to register an RV in the state. Finally, as mentioned before, it's pretty centrally located.

I had arrived in Livingston with a cold that turned into bronchitis, so I stayed a few more days to take care of it. After that, I drove to another RV park near Houston. I hired Blackbird RV, a mobile RV repair service located nearby, to take care of a few minor things and improvements I wanted to make but couldn't do on my own. He did a great job and I've hired him since then for several other things, including fixing my propane tank. While at that RV park, Kathy and Vicki, two women from the Travato group, stopped by to say hello and look at my van. They had ordered a Travato but hadn't received it yet. I gave them a tour and made two new friends. I still bump into them at meet-ups.

So, my first month as a nomad was not stellar. I broke

down emotionally and the van broke down physically. But I was not deterred in the least. I now had a new home and was ready to tackle life on the road.

12

I GET TO DO THIS!

My second month on the road was exactly what I had envisioned for my nomadic life. It was a mixture of awe, excitement, sightseeing, and writing. Early in the month, I went to my first big tourist attraction, the Space Center in Houston. It was on my sightseeing bucket list, and I was blown away by the place. I've since visited it again with a friend.

After visiting friends there, I did something else I'd always wanted to do. I drove along the Gulf of Mexico, right along it, passing through small towns with the ocean often on my right. Although I knew that homes along the Gulf were built on stilts because of storm flooding, I wasn't prepared to see them built so high up. It was amazing and frightening to me that the water could surge so high. At times, the road went inland and over swamps. It was a strange new land for me, and I loved it all.

My first few nights in Louisiana I stayed at the Sam Houston Johnson State Park near Lake Charles. The campground was surrounded by woods and swamps. The first morning, I decided to go for a walk along one of the trails. I had only gone a few yards when I spotted a sign warning about alligators and ticks. *Huh? Alligators? Ticks?* I immediately turned around and took my walk along the paved road that ran through the campground. It circled a large pond. Again, there were alligator warnings. The next morning, I decided to take another walk before leaving the campground. A thick fog had settled low over the ground and it was so creepy, like the opening credits of the TV show, *True Blood*. I was definitely not in Los Angeles any longer.

The next day, I stayed at my first Harvest Hosts location. The first of many. It was the Vermilion Living History Museum. I found a great parking spot next to a small lake and green belt with ducks and squirrels running around. This living museum celebrates the different people who settled this area, like Acadians, Native Americans, Creoles, and African Americans. It was a fascinating place with original structures and replicas to go in and out of and learn about. I love places like this. Over the years, I have returned to this Harvest Hosts location a couple of times and recommended it to other travelers. They also have a restaurant that is only open for lunch and is known for its authentic Cajun food. The next day, I met someone from my fan club for lunch. We had a great time. After lunch, I hit the road for New Orleans.

During my visit to New Orleans, I stayed three nights at the Bayou Segnette State Park campground, which was very nice. It wasn't in New Orleans, but I really wasn't keen on taking my van into the city. I'd been there before and knew how narrow and congested the streets were. Instead, I drove to a ferry terminal, parked the van, and took a ferry across the Mississippi River into the city.

I walked all over New Orleans that day. I stopped in a hair salon to get my hair cut and had a wonderful Cajun lunch. By the end of the day, I could barely walk to the ferry terminal for the trip back. I was exhausted, but happy.

After my time at Bayou Segnette State Park, I drove to Biloxi, Mississippi. I was a day early to check in at Davis Bayou Campground in Ocean Spring, so I spent the night parked in the small lot next to Harrah's Casino. Two other Travatos were parked there, and I got to meet one of the couples.

The next morning, I was the only Travato left in the lot. I couldn't check into my campground yet and it was only about ten miles away, so I took my time and did a little grocery shopping first.

This campground came highly recommended by other Travato owners, and I was delighted with it. I'd booked it for a week. It would be the first time, outside of staying for months at the RV park in California, that I would stay so long in one place. Although not situated on a lake or ocean, it's a compact, well-tended campground that's close to restaurants, shops, services, and attractions. The small town of Ocean Springs is charming. There's a beach with great walking paths and a long pier perfect for strolling and sitting. Although I didn't know it at the time, visiting Davis Bayou Campground would become almost an annual thing, particularly during Christmas. So far, I've been there six times, usually staying a couple of weeks. I fondly refer to it as my *Holiday Home*.

One of the days during my first visit, I went into the historic area of Ocean Springs. I made several stops based on the recommendations of friends. First, I went to the Tato-Nut Donut Shop. They make their donuts with potato flour and they're so light and airy. If you go, get there very early as they sell out quickly. I bought a donut and coffee and sat at a small table outside to enjoy them. While I was there, they sold out and it wasn't even close to noon. I then walked down the street and visited French Kiss Pastrics, another recommendation. Again, a place not to be missed. One of their many specialties are mini cakes. I bought a couple, plus some savory items, and stored them in the van. This is one of the great things about having a camper van. I can buy things that need refrigeration with no concern—just store them in the onboard fridge and go on your way sightseeing. I also visited the lovely Walter Anderson Museum of Art and ran into other travelers I knew.

The last thing I did during my first outing in Ocean Springs was go to the beach. It was a very pretty day. I parked the van along the beach and walked the length of the pier. The crisp ocean air was so enjoyable. Across the bay, I could see Biloxi.

Then, something unexpected happened. I started crying. Not ugly sobs like when the van broke down, or the excited tears the day I left Los Angeles, but a soft weeping of happiness. Waves of amazement washed over me.

I get to do this!

And not just for a few days or a week, but for as long as I wanted. I was living my dream life. I had made it happen. The realization was quite powerful.

To this day, years later, I am still amazed that *I get to do this*, and say those words to myself often when something truly extraordinary or stunning crosses my path. I never want to take this opportunity for granted.

13

A WOMAN LIKE ME

After I left Mississippi, I headed for Alabama. I was scheduled to be a co-guest of honor at two book events. One was in Birmingham, the other in Wetumpka. These two events are co-joined in that they are held at the same time each year and share the authors who attend. I had been to these events a couple of times before, but now I was asked to be a co-guest of honor with the very funny Lee Goldberg. Plus, there would be other authors there I knew very well. I drove to Alabama full of excitement to see so many friends and make new ones.

On the way to Birmingham, I stopped for a few days at Gunter Hill Campground, which was another great camping recommendation by a friend. Check-in was noon and I was very early, so I decided to mark something off my bucket list.

Walking the Edmund Pettus Bridge in Selma was something I'd always wanted to do. Now, I had the chance. It was about forty minutes from the campground. The bridge was the location of Bloody Sunday. On March 7, 1965, Civil Rights Movement marchers crossed the bridge heading from Selma to Montgomery in support of voting rights. When they crossed it, they were met by armed troopers with clubs and tear gas. Many marchers were beaten, some nearly to death, including the late Congressman John Lewis. Every step I took filled my heart with emotions ranging from excitement to pride to rage. I was walking where pioneers of the Civil Rights Movement had walked and bled for equal rights. I was thrilled to see several families walking it as the parents explained the historical significance of the bridge. I recorded my walk across the bridge on my phone and later posted it to my YouTube channel.

Settled into my lovely campsite that afternoon at Gunter Hill Campground, I received a Facebook message from someone saying they were camping right across from me. I assumed it was a reader who recognized my van from its Novel RV signage, which was happening off and on. Instead, it was someone who had looked me up because of those signs. They invited me to their campsite for a drink. Always happy to meet new people, I went.

Here is where things got a bit tense and weird. Before I'd even gotten settled in their extra camp chair, the husband asked, "What's a woman like you doing walking that damn bridge?"

Huh?

I quickly realized a *woman like you* meant *White woman.* I'd never been asked such a question in my life. It stymied me for a few seconds. Then, I answered, saying the Edmund Pettus Bridge was an important historical landmark of civil and voting rights for *all* of us. I half expected an argument, but instead received just a dirty look. I was starting to think that maybe I should make an excuse to return to my van, but decided to stay. I fielded their questions, many asked with an aggressive tone, which ranged from what I thought about Donald Trump's wall to illegal immigration. They even asked me if I was packing (carrying a gun). They had noted my Texas plates, but early in our conversation surmised that I wasn't really from Texas. When I explained that I was a recent transplant to Texas from Los Angeles, they really looked at me in disgust. It was not the first time I'd received such reactions. I quickly learned to stop telling people where I'd recently lived.

In spite of our political differences, the evening ended up being pleasant enough as we moved on to the common ground of travel. However, I wouldn't be honest if I didn't say that when I returned to my van, I was very concerned about the encounter. In the morning, I saw that they had pulled out as planned, but on my picnic table was a strand of solar lights I had admired at their campsite. They had left them with a note saying how nice it was to meet me and they hoped I enjoyed the lights.

This wasn't the first time in my travels that I had come across aggressive behavior from people with different views from my own, nor the last. I don't go around looking for such encounters. Each time, they had discovered me through my signage. Just as my readers were finding me, so were people who weren't fans. A few years later, I was called an *n*-lover because I'd visited so many museums and sites regarding Black history. So far, these situations have all ended well. But like I said earlier, I removed my Novel RV signs from my van just to be safe.

14

DOING MY AUTHOR THING

I had a great time at my author events in Birmingham and Wetumpka, Alabama, and it was so nice to meet up with some of my writer friends, especially some from Los Angeles like Lee Goldberg, who was the other co-guest of honor, and Matt Coyle.

In 2019, I found myself running all over the country fulfilling speaking obligations. This was something I didn't plan well. I was receiving requests from all over, and I tried to group them into regions but still found myself traveling long days to make all of them. I kept telling myself I would do better in 2020. Famous last words. In early 2020, COVID hit and all speaking invitations dried up and have never returned to the way they were.

After leaving the events in the Birmingham and Wetumpka areas, I drove to Monroe, Louisiana, for another event. I had several days to get there, so I spent a few nights in campgrounds working on writing projects. The event in Monroe went very well. Then, I was off to Texas for a bunch of library events in the Tyler area. I have since become very acquainted with Tyler. One of my close friends lives there.

I had a few days before my library events, so decided to camp at Tyler State Park. This is one of the prettiest state parks I have ever visited. A friend who then owned a Travato met me there. However, a big cold front came through with below freezing temperatures. My van was not winterized, but I thought it might be okay because it was going to go above freezing during the day. After one day, my friend, who is from Florida, left because she had not packed for the cold. It was while at this park that I had to break ice in my toilet, as I mentioned in a previous chapter. But once the cold passed, I enjoyed long walks in the park.

A friend had set up the library events in Texas. She went with me to one of them, and I went solo to the others. They were not well attended, but that sometimes happens. I did have a nice group at one of them. At one, no one showed up because severe weather was predicted. The librarian said people had called to apologize for not coming. While I was there, a massive thunderstorm hit with the threat of hail and possible tornadoes. Rain came down in buckets. It got so dark out at one point that the security lights on the outside of the library switched on. But we got through it fine, with no hail or tornadoes. This was one of my first experiences on the road with severe weather, but it would be far from my last.

15

MY FIRST OFFICIAL RALLY

My next author events were not until May and they were in the Pacific Northwest. Between my last author event and those, I had a lot of time to explore as I made my way west, then north. Before heading to the Northwest, I had scheduled a meet-up with other Winnebago owners in Scottsdale, Arizona. It was the first Winnie B BNR, a rally for Winnebago Class B vans, and my first ever rally. But before I got there, I crammed in a lot of adventures. Some were fun and cool. Some were scary.

One of my most exhilarating and one of my most frightening experiences happened on the same day in early March 2019. I crossed off another major bucket list item when I visited Carlsbad Caverns. I still consider it one of the most incredible natural sites I've visited. From the moment I stepped off the elevator seven hundred fifty feet below the surface, and throughout my visit, I was speechless. I'm not sure what I expected. Caverns, for sure, but not of this magnitude and beauty. The trail through the caverns was just over a mile long and each step was filled with awe.

Next comes the scary part of my day, and, like the caverns, something I will never forget. This was when I found myself in the middle of the cyclone bomb weather I detailed in a previous chapter on weather. I still shudder when I remember the two nights I spent in the Walmart parking lot pinned down by the worst winds I've ever experienced. New Mexico is known for their bad winds, but this was like something out of a scary movie. There were moments when the van shook so much that I truly thought it might flip and I would die. I slept in my clothes and dashed in and out of the bathroom. The last thing I wanted was to be blown away with my pants around my ankles.

On the second day in the parking lot, there was a knock on my door. The horrible winds were still raging outside, so I was quite surprised. I looked out my window and saw a man trying not to get blown away. Thinking it might be Walmart's security asking me to move along, I opened my sliding door a tiny bit, but it was very difficult against the wind. No matter what, I was not moving and I was ready to tell him so. But he wasn't security. He was another camper who wanted to know if they could stay in the parking lot. He had to shout to be heard above the wind. He pointed to a camper van near mine, saying it was his and that his wife was inside. At this point, there were more than a dozen of us taking shelter in the parking lot. I assured him that Walmart was not going to send anyone out to shoo us off in this killer wind.

If he only knew that I was initially worried that they might.

The windstorm ended very early the next morning. I knew immediately when it did because it was suddenly quiet and still. After looking outside to confirm everything was safe, I put on shoes and got the hell out of there as soon as it was daylight.

I headed to my next campground, Aguirre Springs, which was near Las Cruces, New Mexico. The campground was recommended by friends. I planned on staying a few days if I liked it. The campsites at Aguirre Springs are on the small side and not very level. It was the first time I had to use my leveling blocks, and it took a bit to get them lined up on my own. Usually, I don't mind being a little off kilter, but this was really sloped. I had a spectacular view from my site and spent two days at my picnic table working, mixed with some mild hiking. On the morning of my third day, I woke up to snow and much lower temperatures. Not a surprise, because after my experience a few days earlier, I now kept a close eye on the weather. The daytime temperature had dropped considerably, but the snow was gone in no time.

On my way into Aguirre Springs Campground, I experienced my first cattle traffic jam. A group of cattle, made up of mostly cows and calves, were crossing the road that wound up the hill to the campground. I came to a stop while I waited for them to pass. To my right was a big bull that was watching me closely. We came to an understanding. I would stay right where I was, making no noise or sudden movements, and he would not charge my van. Eventually, the herd finished crossing the road, with the bull bringing up the rear. I waited until they were all away before moving forward. Years later, a similar thing happened involving a small herd of bison in Custer State Park in South Dakota. While the cows and calves moseyed along in front of my van, taking their sweet time crossing the road, a single bull watched me closely. But I knew the drill.

They moved at their own pace, and I patiently watched until I could safely pass without antagonizing their protector.

The day after the snowstorm, I decided to meet some friends at the City of Rocks in New Mexico. I still had one night left on my stay at Aguirre Springs, but I really wanted to see the City of Rocks and these friends, so I packed up the van and left a day early. Such is the beauty of inexpensive campgrounds. If you change your mind, or need to move on, it is not a big loss.

Made entirely of volcanic rock formations, the City of Rocks was amazing. Even if you're not a camper, try to see it. It's a little bit spooky, like where the spare parts for Stonehenge are stored. There are two kinds of campsites. Some are traditional with power and water, and the others are dry camping among the rock formations. I chose to dry camp near my friends.

I was supposed to stay a few days, but I had to cut it short when my propane ran out and my tank refused to refill. Not the first or last time this would happen. Even an RV repair place could not get it to work. I did manage to stay a couple of days without propane, at least until the nights got very cold. Then, I left and went to an RV park in Casa Grande. The RV park was not far from the meet-up site, and I could use the electric and water hookups to give my van a good scrubbing before heading to the event. And scrub I did. I did laundry, washed floors, and changed sheets. The next day on the way to the meet-up, I even got myself a pedicure. The van and I were all spiffed up and ready for our first official rally.

I wasn't sure what to expect. I only knew there would be a lot of vans there, along with representatives from

Winnebago and other various companies that supplied appliances and items for the vans. One thing I was very excited about was getting a new screen for my van's sliding door. The original screen was just awful. It was always coming off its track and was not very efficient at keeping bugs out. The Canadian company, Rolef, had come up with a design specific to the Travato. As soon as I heard they were going to be at the meet-up, I put in an order for one of their screens. It was pricey, but they installed it on-site and disposed of the old one. I've had it now for years and it has never failed me, except later when I got a cat and she learned how to bypass the screen to escape.

I had already done an article for WinnebaGoLife, but at the rally I was going to interview Sean Gobin, a Travato owner who also operates Warrior Expeditions, a non-profit organization helping former military personnel re-enter civilian life. I really enjoyed interviewing Sean. He uses his Travato as a base camp during the various trips his organization puts on, mostly involving hiking the Appalachian Trail.

The rest of the rally involved attending seminars and Q&A sessions about our vans and traveling in them. I met a lot of new people and got to know some I'd already met better. After the rally, I connected with a couple of friends for lunch. So, the entire experience was wonderful. I don't go to a lot of meet-ups or rallies, even now, but I do recommend to travelers that they attend a couple to learn more and to bond with others. Traveling solo can be lonely at times, and it helps to solidify connections with people with similar interests. I'm always running into people I've met at such events.

After the rally in Arizona, I drove to Twenty-Nine Palms in California, where I visited my great-nephew, Josh, who was at the Marine base there. Early on in my journey, it was becoming clear how useful it was to have wheels I could also call home. It made it so easy to meet up with friends and family, and to make new friends. No need for a hotel or a rental car. No crowded airports. And you brought along your own bathroom!

16

THE PRODIGAL NOMAD RETURNS

Soon after the meet-up, I returned to California for the first time in three months. Since I had left, I had traveled to seven states, spoken at seven book events, been through two snowstorms, one hailstorm, and two days of hurricane-strength winds. Plus, I'd broken up ice in my toilet. I'd seen an alligator in the wild, many species of squirrels, longhorn cattle, cranes, ducks, many cardinals, many cacti, and gobs-macking rock formations and caverns.

After my visit with Josh, I returned to the Los Angeles area to visit friends. I had a great time, which included a trip to Duke's Restaurant in Malibu where my friend Jennifer and I were treated to seeing a pod of dolphins during lunch. While in Southern California, I managed to get into a campground on a beach for three nights, and I spent one night at the home of friends. Now, I wouldn't think of staying at that beach campground and paying such a high nightly price, which has increased since then. But as I noted under the money section, the first year I went a little crazy. I've since learned how to get more bang for my buck on the road. I've also since stayed in much prettier places for free or near free.

All my friends welcomed me *home* with open arms. But was it home? Not any longer. In just three months, I had pulled away from that fast lifestyle and kicked it to the curb. I hated the traffic, the noise, and the expense. After just a few days in Southern California, I was longing for the peace of the road and open spaces. This is from a woman who had spent most of her life in bustling cities.

From Southern California, I headed north. My destination was the Pacific Northwest, where I had some speaking engagements, another meet-up, and a volunteer obligation. Along the way, I was going to stop near San Jose and visit several friends. Except for one night I spent in Morro Bay, I was having a lot of trouble finding campgrounds along my route in California. Most were filled up, and others were ultra expensive, especially those near San Jose. I hit upon a plan. I booked two nights at an inexpensive but decent motel. It worked out great. I used my van to travel the few miles to see my friends, then returned to the motel at night. Those two nights cost me less than one night at one of the RV resorts in the area, and I got a free breakfast. So, if you're traveling in an RV and having trouble getting a place to stay, don't rule something like this out. The next couple of nights, I was fortunate enough to stay with other van owners in their driveway. Friends always feel bad when they can't accommodate me in my van due to space limitations or HOA rules, but I understand and always manage to find something.

Friends also assume that I'm dying to sleep inside their home, use their shower, and laundry facilities. Not so. If you ask many of us who have rigs with bathrooms, we will tell you that we prefer our own accommodations. I have a shower. It may be small, but it gets the job done very well, and I don't have to pack and haul clothes and toiletries inside someone's home. Once in a while, I'll opt for a campground or truck stop shower. This is usually when I feel the need to stand under hot water for a long time, but I prefer my own shower for its convenience. The same goes for my bed. I sleep better in my own bed in my van. It's *my* bed and my home. As for laundry, I much prefer to go to a laundromat where I can do multiple loads at once and get it all done in about two hours or less. It is much more efficient than doing one load at a time in someone's home. So, if you offer a nomad friend the use of your home and they turn down your generous gesture, don't feel hurt. Like most of you, we prefer our own digs.

My last stay with Travato friends was just north of San Francisco. From there, I decided to take the Pacific Coast Highway north. I'd driven it from San Francisco to San Diego, but never the north section. It was glorious and the scenery was incredible, even if the hair-pin turns and hills were a bit daunting. I was moving along at a good pace, so I decided to find a decent campground. I still didn't have working propane, a problem that would plague me again a few years later, so I needed hookups since the weather was windy and chilly. I found a nice small rustic campground near Caspar Bay and stayed there a couple of days. During this time, I got a lot of writing done and took walks to the beach during the day.

Next stop: The Pacific Northwest!

17

THE PACIFIC NORTHWEST

It was in Ashland, Oregon, that I got my first taste of nasty camping etiquette. I was at Emigrant Lake Campground and had purchased a campsite for a week. I picked one that was available and paid for it. The camp host put a reserved sign on my post. All was fine. I'd even alerted the host that I'd be in and out during that time, and she said that would be fine, just to make sure my tag remained on my post.

Interesting fact about Emigrant Lake: Beneath it is the town of Klamath Junction. The reservoir lake was formed in the 1920s, but in the 1960s it was expanded and the tiny town of Klamath Junction was abandoned and submerged.

When traveling in a van, that van is also your only mode of transportation. So, after settling into a campsite, you might have to leave it to sightsee or to get supplies. I'd done this before with no issue. The tag on the post says the campsite is unavailable. However, upon my return after visiting friends in town, someone had hijacked my primo campsite. Someone with a big trailer had ignored the posted reserved sign, moved in, and set up their camp. They were gone when I returned, or I would have given them an earful. I'd paid over two hundred dollars for the week at that site.

The ranger came by and heard me out, saying that, sadly, this happened a lot. He asked if I would be okay moving to another site for the rest of my stay. I said yes, but it was a holiday weekend. The place was nearly booked solid except for single nights, and I would not accept being moved every day to accommodate the remainder of my time. The ranger asked me to move into the day-use area while they sorted it out. I said no way, feeling that if I was out of sight, nothing would get done. I dug in my heels. The ranger was very nice and calm, and he was trying to resolve the issue without too much confrontation. But in the paraphrased words of an iconic Glenn Close character, I would not be ignored (Just so you know, I would never boil a bunny. Not even for a primo campsite!).

Other campers were watching this go down. The ranger and I found my missing reserved sign. It had been removed and stuck behind the reservation information for the people coming into the site after me. It had been willfully moved and hidden. On the top of the pile was a handwritten reserved sign for the hijackers. The camp host also came by and confirmed that the site was mine and that she had put up the reserved sign herself.

The ranger went around looking for a site with three open nights, which was the remainder of my time there. There were none. But he did think a cancellation had come in for the site two down from my original site. He asked if it were open, would I be happy with it? Sure, I told him. I didn't want to be nasty about it. I just wanted my remaining three nights, with a lake view, that I paid for. So, while he went off to confirm the cancellation, I pulled my van into that site. It was identical to the one I had, even with pretty much the same view. I sat at the picnic table, waiting for the outcome. He assured me if there wasn't any availability, he would tell the campsite hijackers to move, but he hoped it wouldn't come to that. He also asked me not to confront the people if they returned. He said to let him discuss it with them. I promised. After all, I was pretty upset, and I really didn't want a scene, just a nice campsite for the next three nights.

The ranger returned and announced that the people in the site where I was parked had canceled their reservation. He took off their reservation sign and replaced it with mine. I returned to the picnic table and tried to calm down. I wanted to reclaim the peace of earlier in the day, but frankly, my day had been ruined by this. I know, I should not have let it, but I did.

The campsite thieves returned right after the ranger left. True to my word, I didn't engage with them. The camp host joined me and we chatted. She was about my age and had been full-time RVing for a few years. She confirmed that this type of stuff happened all the time and it was difficult to resolve. She turned out to be a mystery fan and we chatted about books. It helped me calm down. We were interrupted by the husband of the site jumpers calling her over to my old site. She went, and I saw that the ranger was there, along with another camper who had watched my meltdown. They were having a loud discussion about campsite theft, with the ranger and camp host remaining calm and explaining to the husband how that site had been reserved prior to their arrival. The husband was arguing that it was rightfully their site because I wasn't physically there when they arrived. The other camper was complaining how this happened all the time and wasn't right. I stayed out of it, as promised.

I learned later from the ranger that those folks were known troublemakers in the campground. He told me to stay away from them during the rest of my stay, which I did. But I doubt I'll ever camp at that campground again, even though it was lovely. The camp host and ranger, although both nice, had allowed themselves to be bullied and intimidated rather than doing the right thing. When bullies are not stopped, they continue their ugly ways.

Similar things have happened to other van friends, especially at first-come-first-served campgrounds. People say to leave out an old chair or tablecloth or other inexpensive items to let people know the site is taken. But friends have done that, only to return to find their tables or chairs in the back of someone's pickup and their site stolen. I often use an expandable caution cone with OCCUPIED written on it to alert people I'm only gone for a short time, but one time I did return to find my site unoccupied and my cone stolen. Generally, campers do not steal from other campers, but there are always a few who ruin it for everyone else.

My time in Ashland was not all campground drama. I got to see my friends, Pam and Darrell, and I even attended a writers' group that Pam runs. My friend, Morgan, also lived in Ashland. She was another writer. We spent a great deal of time together during my stay. After the issue of the campsite switch, Morgan would drive out and pick me up so I didn't have to drive my van into town. It worked out pretty well. Sadly, that was the last time I ever saw Morgan. She had been battling cancer for a very long time and passed away just over a year later.

My van has allowed me to say goodbye to several people. Besides seeing Morgan in Oregon, I was able to travel to visit a favorite uncle in Massachusetts a few months before he passed away, also of cancer. I've been able to visit a few elderly family members, with the van making it much easier to spend time with them, as well as other friends and family.

I spent a great deal of time in the Pacific Northwest my first and second year of my journey. After leaving Emigrant Lake Campground, I headed north. I stayed with more Travato owners and visited a tulip farm in full bloom while still in Oregon. If you get a chance to do that, don't miss it.

I was heading up to Fort Flagler Campground in Washington where I had beautiful views of Port Townsend Bay, which feeds into Puget Sound. Not too many miles across the water is Victoria, British Columbia. To my left was Indian Island Naval Base. The camp host told me they see submarines and ships in the bay all the time.

The drive to Fort Flagler was very beautiful. The weather was in the 50s and clear. Highway 101 curves along the Hood Canal much of the way before cutting inland. Both sides of the road are lined with thick woods, only breaking for occasional settlements and vacation homes. Further along, you leave the hilly road for farmland.

I caught a break on this portion of my trip. I tried once again to get propane into my propane tank. This time, the valve unstuck and I was able to fill it. I was so happy because unless I was plugged in, I had no way to get heat and hot water without the propane and it was getting chillier the more north I traveled. Now, I could dry camp in comfort again. I would not be so lucky in a couple of years. In the fall of 2022, my propane tank failed again, but this time the valve was not stuck inside. It had broken off. I was without propane for a long time before I found some place in my travels that could fix it. I ended up returning to Texas and Bluebird RV for the repair.

The meet-up I was attending in Washington was being

held in the group area of the Fort Flagler Campground. I'd arrived a few days earlier and camped in the public area, during which time I wrote quite a bit. When it was time, I moved over to the group area and met mostly with folks I'd never met before, several of which became very good friends.

During the days of the meet-up, it got very cold. The wind whipped right through me. I don't like wearing heavy jackets, but I do carry one. I put it to good use that weekend. I've only had to use it a few times in the five years I've been a nomad, both times in Washington.

If you're planning a long journey on the road, don't forget to prepare accordingly. I left California without any jackets, just depending on sweaters and sweatshirts. Before one year was up, I owned a rain jacket and a cold weather parka. Both can be folded to take up very little space in the van. I find I use the rain jacket all the time.

After the meet-up was over, I went back to the general camping area of Fort Flagler and stayed several more days. During this time, I was writing up a storm every day while looking at the water. It was heaven. Since then, my favorite writing locations are those where I can see a river, lake, or the ocean. It both inspires and soothes me.

I was juggling a lot of different projects. My former publisher had given me the rights back to some of my books and I was busy editing and getting them ready for re-publication. The two vampire books were done and just needed new covers, which I had ordered. Now, I could start working on the other books that needed to be gone through for re-publication. Later in the year, I received the rights back on the rest of the books under this publisher. I was also working on my novel, *Finding Zelda*. This poor book was taking a backseat to everything else.

Each day, I worked hard on my writing, except for one day when I went into the nearby town to do laundry and some grocery shopping. When I returned to the campsite, I checked into a new site that had an even more spectacular view of the bay. Once settled, I kept my nose to the grindstone and my eye on my great view. One day, the camp host came by to check on me. He and his wife were worried because they hadn't seen me in a few days. I thanked him for their concern and explained that I was a writer juggling a couple of deadlines. In the midst of all this, I was still writing for WinnebaGoLife and had just turned in an article. I was a writing machine in my early time on the road, keeping the same breakneck pace I had before my life changed.

I still had time before my next speaking engagements, so I decided to tour the Pacific Northwest a little more. From Fort Flagler, I drove to the Olympic National Forest in Washington and spent a couple of days there. It was so beautiful and different to camp in the woods instead of by the bay. I continued my writing routine everyday, breaking only to take daily walks. One thing that worried me were the posters the park put up warning about cougars in the area, stating not to walk or bike alone and to always carry a stick. I am a city girl, so that scared the tar out of me. But I continued my short walks, staying on the road and not going on the wooded trails. And I carried a walking pole with me. Years later, I am still scared of most wildlife, although I love seeing it and listening to coyotes at night.

I'd never really explored the Pacific Northwest, but now I had my chance. I had two speaking commitments in Washington and a very special volunteering commitment in Oregon. Outside of those, my time was my own. Before going to the Olympic National Forest, I visited Port

Townsend. After I left the campground, I went to Port Angeles to do some errands. Every night if I had connectivity, I would pore over possible places to see between my scheduled engagements. I still do this years later. I'm always discovering new and different things to see.

My next campground was going to be Kalaloch Campground overlooking the Pacific Ocean. On the way there, I visited Crescent Lake, which was larger than I expected and stunning. Kalaloch Campground was very nice and first-come-first-served until the middle of May. I couldn't find an open spot overlooking the ocean, but found one that was nice and fairly close to it. I got acquainted with some people camping nearby. One was a young woman from Australia who was in one of the best coastline sites. She was leaving the next day and told me she would give me a heads-up when she left so I could snag her spot. Because of her generosity and the camp host's flexibility, I got to spend five days with a stunning view of the rugged Pacific Northwest coastline. I spent the days writing, walking, and enjoying my gorgeous view. I would sit in my camp chair in the sun and listen to audiobooks. I ate many of my meals at my picnic table and cooked several outside. This was the life I had dreamed of, and it was coming true.

Unfortunately, I hit another snag with my van. I'd had my generator oil changed in Port Angeles, but when I tried to turn on my generator, it wouldn't work. I had not tried to use it since the oil change, but now I needed it. My coach batteries were getting low, which could be expected after sitting still for several days. They were being charged by my solar panels, but some days were not very sunny. The generator would have charged them right up. Fortunately, I made it through my stay at Kalaloch, and my drive after leaving the campground put a nice charge on the batteries again. My propane was working, but now my generator was not. I also had to unplug my galley sink. I was quickly learning that it is always something with RVs. Not to say they are full of issues, but you learn what to do in a pinch, and you have to be constantly aware of your systems.

From Kalaloch, I drove down the Washington coast into Oregon. Highway 101 along the coast is stunning, and something everyone should see. I am still amazed at the way big pines cling to the side of the cliffs. Much of my drive was again in the Olympic National Forest. I spent the night at the Blue Heron French Cheese Company in Oregon, a Harvest Hosts location. I met a few other travelers there. It's always nice to meet others on the road, especially other single women who are putting themselves out there to follow their dream.

The next night, my spidey-sense was on full alert. I had planned to stay at a specific campground but had not made reservations. When I arrived, I found it full, even on a Monday night. I located a Washington State Park not too far away on one of my camping apps and went there. There was no one in the office, only rules and information on how to self-book a stay posted on a bulletin board. I drove around the campground looking for a suitable site. There were many open sites, but the ones that were occupied looked very sketchy. The campground was full of broken-down RVs and car campers. I even saw a couple of eviction notices on a few RVs. My spidey-sense was going nuts. I ended up checking my camping app again and discovered that I could stay for free at a casino not too far away. I later learned from other travelers that the campground I had visited had been overrun with homeless people and squatters, with the state having little control over it. The casino, on the other hand, was not only free, but much safer. So, always listen to your spidey-sense.

The next day, I wanted to drive until I was close to my scheduled speaking engagement, which was not very far, but I needed a place to hang out and spend the night. It was also raining steadily, so doing much sightseeing was out of the question. I ended up doing something that I now often do when I find myself with time to kill before heading to an overnight spot. I found a local park and spent the day there. The park was lovely but, unfortunately, I couldn't spend the night there. I parked with a view of a small lake and spent the day writing. Being a rainy day, not many people were there. The park was open until late, but around dinner time, I moved to my overnight spot.

Here is my eighty-mile round trip error. Before settling in at the park, I'd decided to stay at a truck stop about forty miles up the road, very close to where my speaking gig was to be held. When I got to the truck stop, I discovered that they no longer allowed overnight parking for RVs. I had used locations of this particular truck stop chain before, but had been finding them less open to RV parking. After gassing up my van, I went inside and asked about staying the night. I was told that I would be towed if I did. I ended up driving back forty miles to the town where I had spent the day in the park, and spent the night in the parking lot of their local small Walmart. This Walmart also had signs for no overnight parking, but when I went inside and asked about it, they were very nice and gave me permission. I no longer use that national truck stop chain for anything, not even for gas. But I did shop at that Walmart and even got a haircut there that evening. If you are a traveler, do support the companies that support you. Whether I stay at a

Walmart, a restaurant, or a truck stop, I give them my busi-ness if they give me a safe place to stay.

I had two speaking engagements in the Pacific North-west. Both went off without a hitch. I'd been doing such events for years, but now I started seeing a change in my presentations. Before, people engaged me to talk about my books and my writing career. Now, they wanted to know more about my travels. I would still pitch my novels, but most of the questions from the audiences were about my new lifestyle. My first gig in the Pacific Northwest was to a group of female entrepreneurs. Here, I talked about how I had rebranded my writing career and expanded it to include travel writing. From then on, my speaking focus was a blend of my fiction, non-fiction, and my nomadic life. Like my lifestyle, my presentations had to be flexible and ever changing to meet the curiosity of my audiences.

18

NEW WAYS TO GIVE

After my time in Washington, I was through with speaking engagements for a while. I drove down to Oregon and visited with my friend, Larry, who is also a nomad. Larry is a freelance contractor and handyman who also does a lot of pet and house-sitting. For a couple of days, I stayed in the driveway of the place where he was currently staying. This is where I got the idea of trying my hand at house-sitting as well. Being new to the nomadic lifestyle, I was eager to try new things to add to my experiences. I signed up on one of the agencies Larry used and soon had my first gig, but it was not for another month due to my schedule.

After saying goodbye to Larry, I went to meet-up with other Travato friends for a volunteer week at Camp Attitude, a summer camp for special needs children. The children who come to Camp Attitude have very serious health issues, and are the ones other camps for special needs kids must turn away because of the complexity of their needs. One of my friends had volunteered there the year before, getting the camp ready for the summer season. There had to be about eight vans there this year, plus one travel trailer.

We were given daily tasks, such as cleaning cabins, painting, and gardening. At night, after cleaning up, we would sit around and visit. It was hard work, but a wonderful time and felt so rewarding. I even used a power washer for the first time. We were there a week, staying in the RV sites that the camp maintains for the families of the campers. One of the last days, we took an afternoon off and went to a nearby lake. Many brought their kayaks, while some of us, like me, lounged on the beach. It was a glorious afternoon. It was sad to say goodbye to my friends when our time was up.

Before leaving Camp Attitude, one of my friends and I agreed to spearhead the following year's clean-up crew. Many of those who had been there wanted to return. We were excited about promoting it for 2020 and having even more volunteers. Unfortunately, the pandemic caused the camp to remain closed that year and the next, so we never got a chance to return.

There are many ways for RVers to give back. There are projects like this, plus several travelers I know sign up for Habitat for Humanity worksites. Others do special projects around the country through religious affiliations. Some have used their vans to help bring supplies to evacuees fleeing fires and storms. It really helps to have your own little movable house so that you're not putting a burden on the communities you're serving.

19

PET AND HOUSE-SITTING

After Camp Attitude, I headed to my first pet-sitting job. I didn't get paid for these jobs, but did have a place to park my RV and a nice home to live in for a while. Not that I wanted to get off the road, but it was nice to live in a sticks-and-bricks place for a bit. Although, I still prefer my van over someone else's home.

My first pet-sitting job was for a breeder of springer spaniels who needed someone to look after her home and other dogs while she took one of her dogs to be bred. She and her husband planned to be gone for three to five days. They had a beautiful compound in Idaho with a very nice kennel. My job was to let the other dogs out of the kennel in the morning, feed them, play with them, and clean up after them. The dogs were allowed to run free on the fenced-in property all day and were very good when it was time to go back to the kennel in the evening. I had to care for five dogs. Yes, five bouncy springer spaniels. It was a lot of work, but the animals were so sweet and playful. All five were females and each had a great personality. In spite of the work, I enjoyed spending my days with them. Often, I would write on the back patio and they would sprawl on the floor under the table near me. One, an older dog, was the only one allowed to stay in the house at night. If I watched TV, sometimes she would get up on the sofa with me. Whenever I went into my van to do some chores, one of the younger dogs would hop inside and sprawl on the floor while I took care of things. The owners returned on the fourth day. I missed the dogs when I left.

My next pet-sitting job was unexpected and on the heels of the first one. I was contacted on the pet/house-sitting site by a couple whose scheduled sitter had bailed on them at the last minute. It was in Ogden, Utah. Since the other people came home a day early, I consented to drive like crazy to get to this other home in Utah to save their vacation. They were planning on traveling in their travel trailer for a couple of weeks, but no longer took their dog with them because the animal was old and deaf and couldn't get in or out of the trailer on her own. The dog's name was Lexi and she was so sweet, except when it came to other dogs. She was very easy to care for and loved her twice-a-day walks around the neighborhood park.

I could tell the owners were a bit leery of me since they didn't know me and I had just started pet-sitting. They had planned three weeks for their trip, but told me they would only be gone one week. During the first week, one of their neighbors came by to see how I was doing, no doubt encouraged by a call from my clients. I must have passed muster because they ended up taking the entire three weeks for their travels. In the meantime, I got a whole lot of writing done. Sometimes, I would write at their patio table with Lexi nearby. Other times, I wrote at the kitchen table. The animal was never far from me.

Another benefit of being in one place for a longer time

is to be able to get shopping and services done, which is easier when you aren't constantly on the move. While in Ogden, I met up with friends who lived not very far away. I also got my oil changed, a haircut, and my second tattoo. I ordered a few things from Amazon and caught up on laundry.

In all, I have done five pet-sitting jobs. One was in Batavia, Illinois, with quite a character of a terrier and two cats, and another in Virginia with a young, rambunctious dog that wore me out. They were all enjoyable.

After the one in Virginia, I didn't accept any more pet-sitting jobs. They were being offered, but only by people who wanted a sitter in very cold places while they went on vacation in warmer climes. Uh, no. I spent my winters in warmer places, too, and I had a lot of plans for the rest of 2019.

In 2020, I adopted a cat and decided my pet-sitting days were over for good. My final pet/house-sitting job took place at the end of 2020 and into early 2021, which I will discuss later in the next section since it has a lot to do with the pandemic.

Many nomads find pet/house-sitting a great way to break up their routine. There are several agencies that connect sitters with clients. I believe some allow you to charge for your services. The one I was with didn't, although a couple clients gave me a tip. If you are a traveler and think this might work for you, do your research and check the references of the companies. And make sure you know upfront what is expected of you. Sometimes, the clients are not forthcoming on how much work will be involved. You may think it's just a gentle dog you're caring for, then find out once it's too late that you're expected to take care of a small barnyard. Some clients feel it's free labor and take advantage of the sitters, not fully disclosing what is expected of them. And make sure they have a place for you to park your RV. I was all set to do one job and had confirmed that they had parking for my van in their driveway, only to learn soon before the start of the job that I would have to find a place to park my van while there. I canceled and did not feel one bit bad about it.

20

CITY GIRL MEETS WILDLIFE

Shortly after my pet-sitting in Utah, I drove to the Grand Tetons National Park. I had it in my head to spend the 4th of July weekend there. The national campground I wanted was first-come-first-served. I landed there on July 3rd and was lucky enough to land a great campsite, where I stayed for several days. Grand Tetons National Park quickly became one of my favorite national parks. Even now, it is second only to Glacier National Park in my list of parks. Of course, I've not seen all of the national parks, but I'm working on it. There is something so majestic about the way the Grand Tetons rise up into the blue sky, often ringed by clouds.

On July 4th, very early in the morning, I took off from camp to travel the very long driving loop around the park. Over four hours later, I returned to camp exhausted but excited. I was glad I'd struck out early. The pullouts for taking photos were not crowded. There were people there, just like me, trying to avoid the holiday crowds, and the photo opportunities were incredible. Clouds surrounded the mountains like fluffy fur collars. At one stop, elk grazed

in a meadow. At Jackson Lake Dam, I took a glorious shot of
the mountains mirrored in Jackson Lake. It was all spectacular. At another stop, I took a short hike along a trail on the
edge of Jenny Lake.

I was heading back in the direction of my campground
when I noticed a couple of vehicles ahead of me had come
to a halt. The road was straight and clear, but when I got
closer I saw the issue. There were bison getting ready to
cross the road. To my left, one massive beast was waiting, as
if for a light to change. When the cars stopped in both direc-
tions, he started across with two others following him. The
day before, I had seen my first bison in the wild when I
came into the park. It was part of a large herd grazing off in
the distance. But these three were very close. It was the
perfect ending to a perfect Fourth of July.

I have since seen hundreds of bison up close. Some have
been a little too close for comfort, but if you don't bother
them and are patient as they cross the road or walk alongside of it, you're usually fine. At least, I've not had any bad
experiences with them and I've been close enough in my
van to almost touch them as they passed me by. In my years
on the road, I have witnessed many stupid actions by
tourists with regard to bison. Every year, people get gored or
thrown by these majestic animals because they get too close
or bother them. You simply do not pet the fluffy cows! Nor
do you honk your horn at them. Or try to nudge them along
with your vehicle. You simply sit quietly and wait them out.

One of my last days in the campground, the camp host
dropped by and asked me if I'd seen the bear. *Bear!* He said
that my neighbor had seen one snuffling around the back of
my van that very morning. He explained it was a young
female that often wandered through the campground early
in the morning looking for food dropped by campers. So, a

bear had been just a few feet from where I was sleeping? I still have not seen a bear in the wild, but when I do, I would rather it not be that close.

Following the Grand Tetons, I drove a few miles north and visited Yellowstone National Park. I didn't stay in the park, but I spent the day visiting Old Faithful and then traveling through the eastern side of the massive place. Along the way, I saw so many beautiful things, including a herd of elk. I also saw more bison. I'd like to return one day and tour the rest of the park.

Once I got out of Yellowstone, I entered Shoshone National Forest. It was breathtaking, with stunning high cliffs to my left and beautiful rivers and creeks to my right. Every bend in the road treated me to more gorgeous views.

Finally, I got to Cody, Wyoming, where I was going to spend the night. The next day, I visited the Buffalo Bill Cody Museum. This is an excellent museum that has many more displays than just about Cody. I highly recommend it. For lunch, I met up with a woman who's in the Travato group on Facebook. Toni didn't have a van yet, but she was looking to get one soon. We had a nice lunch and I gave her a tour of my van. Toni is now a very good friend, has a van of her own, and can be found zooming around the country in search of perfect kayaking.

The last thing I visited in Wyoming was Devil's Tower, the famous landmark featured in the movie, *Encounters of the Third Kind*. That was pretty impressive, except when I got there it was so crowded that they were only letting so many vehicles up to the parking lot at the base. The prediction was a three-hour wait, so I moved on after taking photos from below.

My travels next took me into South Dakota. I stopped at a campground in Spearfish to meet my friend, Laura, another full-timer, then it was on to Rapid City. I'd planned to go into Deadwood, but there was a storm rolling in and I wanted to get to Rapid City, where I planned on spending the night. I did eventually get to Deadwood, but it was a few years later.

The storm caught up with me when I was about twenty miles from my destination. It was so bad that I pulled into a rest stop to wait out the worst of it. It was a humdinger, with lightning and thunder and rain so heavy it sounded like rocks hitting the van roof.

The plan was to spend the night at the Cabela's parking lot in Rapid City. When I reached there, the storm was over and it was lovely out. I was even able to have my sliding door open to enjoy the afternoon. I also took this opportunity to slip into Cabela's and buy myself a decent rain jacket. I already had a heavy jacket for cold weather, but no rain jacket. When I came out of the store, there was another Travato next to mine. To my delight, it was Pat and Terry, whom I had met before.

The next morning, I took off to see Mount Rushmore and Custer State Park. Custer State Park, which is considered a top wildlife refuge, has a driving loop that enables people to view their animals, providing the animals are out and about. The park is beautiful, too. I got there as soon as the park opened since most wildlife come out early in the morning. The first animal I saw was a lone elk standing so still I first thought it was a statue. Then, he turned his beautiful head and looked at me. Next, I turned a corner and came upon a small herd of young bison. They were scattered all about the road. Most of them were cows and calves, but there was one huge bull who kept an eye on me. He came so close to my van that if I'd had a passenger, they would have been able to touch him. He let me know through his unmoving stare that he would not tolerate any funny business with his herd. I stayed right where I was until everyone moved across the road. There was one young calf that stood in the road and was very curious about my vehicle. He came very close and I worried that might trigger the bull, but it didn't. The youngster scampered away, and soon I was able to move very slowly down the road.

The wildlife loop through Custer State Park was so much fun. I stopped often to take photos of the scenery, as well as animals. I came across another roadblock about halfway through the drive. There were several cars stopped that were coming from the other direction. In the narrow road was a herd of wild donkeys. Donkeys were also along the sides of the road. Although not as menacing as that bison bull, you still do not touch or aggravate them. They are wild animals, not pets. A good kick to your vehicle can do a lot of damage. I had to put up my window because one of them wanted to stick his head inside. Very slowly, cars moved forward, encouraging the donkeys to move out of the way, which they did in their own good time.

From Custer State Park, I drove to Mount Rushmore. Frankly, I expected to be rather underwhelmed by this monument. Instead, I was very moved. Yes, I understand the issues regarding the theft of the land it is built on from Indigenous people, but I was still blown away by the size and art of the mountainside.

If you have ever driven along highways in South Dakota, you have seen the ubiquitous signs for Wall Drug in Wall, South Dakota. For that matter, Wall Drug signs can be found along any highway in the area. The farthest official sign is in Wyoming, nearly four hundred miles from the store itself. Several scenes in the movie *Nomadland*, took place at Wall Drug. If you're a traveler, you must see

Wall Drug at least once in your travels. For me, it was a one-and-done thing.

Wall Drug is a sprawling tourist attraction of many storefronts that have melded together over the years. Besides having food and a soda fountain, they have every souvenir and bric-a-brac known to man and coveted by tourists. There is even a chapel on the premises. It is a true South Dakota experience.

From Wall Drug, I drove to the Badlands. I'd been wanting to camp there, but it was super hot and even worse in the park. Instead, I drove up a dirt road to some dispersed camping on the cliff overlooking the Badlands known as The Wall. This is great free camping if it's not raining. If it is raining, the road turns to mud. Many a camper has gotten stuck and had to be towed out of ruts there. The views are spectacular from The Wall and there is always a breeze, if not heavy winds. It was still hot up there, but not as bad with the wind. I stayed a few days, at least until a storm moved in. Then, I got out of there before the roads became a mess. I have stayed at The Wall on a couple of occasions, always with incredible views and heavy wind.

I toured the Badlands two years later, taking the Badlands Loop Road from the Pinnacles Entrance to the Northeast Entrance. It's a spectacular, other-worldly place. The rock formations, cliffs, and the colors of the rocks easily make you think you are on the moon or some other planet. Near the Pinnacles Entrance, there is often a large herd of bison. During my drive through the Badlands, I also saw pronghorn sheep, eagles and hawks, and prairie dogs. It was a remarkable experience.

Also on my list of things to see in South Dakota was the Dignity sculpture and the Corn Palace. The full name of Dignity is Dignity of Earth and Sky. It's a fifty-foot, twelve-ton, gorgeous statue of a Native woman with a flowing blanket. The sculpture is made of stainless steel and is located at a large rest stop outside the town of Chamberlain. The view of the Missouri River from there is breathtaking.

The Corn Palace in Mitchell was very interesting and is a huge tourist draw. The outside is adorned with murals made of dried corn. They use different colors of dried corn for the different colors in the murals. This is a venue used for concerts and sports events. When those aren't going on, the main floor is a huge souvenir shop. Sitting in the theater seats a few levels up from the floor, you can see the murals that line the walls and above the stage very clearly. They depict life in South Dakota over the years. The outside mural is changed every year. It is a bit corny (pun intended), but definitely worth checking out as an example of excellent folk art.

21

IF IT'S JULY, IT MUST BE IOWA

From South Dakota, I traveled to Forest City, Iowa, and to my first GNR. This is the annual Grand National Rally put on by Winnebago in Forest City each July. I have attended this event three years now. Hundreds of Winnebago RVs, trailers, and vans converge on the fairgrounds for a week of activities and information. There are concerts, special speakers, parties, and plenty of fun. It's like a summer camp for adults. In fact, it's now officially called Camp Winnebago. I'm not much into crowds, but I've learned to enjoy the fellowship of these types of gatherings.

Like most things, the first time is always special. Once the van was settled in its spot at GNR with the Winnie Bs, the van club, I got out and started meeting people. Some I knew from earlier meet-ups, but most I only knew by name through the online Travato group. Now, I had the chance to meet them in person. I also got to meet many Winnebago people, including the people behind WinnebaGoLife.

There were many activities during the week, but my favorite thing was sitting around in our camp chairs getting to know one another. There were card games and trivia, and several brought musical instruments and played for us. One night was a Row Party. At the annual Row Party, the different clubs and sections of the rally decorate their spaces and are judged on their efforts. They also hand out goodies with some relevance to their state or type of club. It is not unlike trick-or-treating.

While at GNR, I also visited the Winnebago Service Center and had a few things fixed on my van. It was nothing major, but they did get my generator going again and took care of a few other items.

Weather in Iowa in July is no joke. The second day we were there, during pre-rally time, we were hit with a nasty thunderstorm, and even tornado warnings. Other years, the weather has been stiflingly hot. But most of the time I was there that first year, it was pretty nice, except for the occasional rain.

During my first GNR, the Winnie Bs caravanned to Charles City, Iowa, with some Winnebago representatives, including Ruff Garfin, the then Product Manager over Winnebago's Class B camper vans. We overnighted in a large parking lot by the river and got together for dinner. It was fun to watch people stare as about eighty camper vans traveled along together. The next morning, we caravanned to the Winnebago facility in Charles City, where we were treated to tours of the cabinet factory and the van factory. It was so interesting to see how our beloved vans were created and assembled.

Life in the Winnie B section of GNR was fun and easy. One day, I gave a presentation about writing on the road. It went very well. The next day, I was on a panel regarding full-time RVing. It was another successful topic. The back door of my van was acting up and my friend Tom fixed it. It had been fixed before by a dealer, but promptly broke again.

Tom's fix is still working all these years later. At the Winnie B annual meeting, I was elected as secretary. I remained secretary for a few years. The night of the Row Party, I had my first Jell-O shots. Yes, my first. They were made with lime Jell-O and moonshine, and I loved them. During all this fun, I was still writing every day.

Soon, it was time to say goodbye to everyone and get back on the road. It was a time of both sadness and excitement.

My first stop after GNR was Clear Lake, Iowa, to visit the Surf Ballroom where Buddy Holly had his last performance before dying in a plane crash just miles away. After seeing the ballroom, I made my way to the crash site.

On February 3, 1959, Buddy Holly, Ritchie Valens, and The Big Bopper all died in a small plane crash, along with the pilot. The plane plunged into a cornfield shortly after takeoff. The crash site was easy to find. It is along a rural gravel road that runs through acres of farmland. The owner of the field maintains a narrow path from the road to the site. It's easy to identify the site from the road as there is a large replica of the thick, black glasses Holly wore. At the site itself are memorials and things left by fans, even today.

After a night spent in a casino parking lot, I visited the Spam Museum in Austin, Minnesota, right over the border with Iowa. It was the only thing in Minnesota I saw my first year, but I've been back to that lovely state many times since.

The Spam Museum was a hoot! There were a lot of interactive displays, and even a fun area for children. It tells the history of Spam, but also of the Hormel company. Hormel, of course, is a huge food manufacturer, and Spam is one of their products. But most of the displays were about Spam, such as how it came about, the flavors, its use over the years in the military, and how widespread it is in the world now. Many of the displays are even quite funny, like the Monty Python Spamalot display. We ate a lot of Spam growing up, and I dislike it, but this was one of my favorite, fun museums.

After slipping back into Iowa, I visited a lot of quirky things for photo opportunities, then another museum. This time, it was the John Deere Tractor and Engine Museum in Waterloo, Iowa. It detailed the history of early engines used for agriculture and the John Deere Company. It was very interesting and a great learning experience.

From Iowa, I headed into Missouri.

22

VISITS WITH MARK TWAIN, POPEYE, AND SUPERMAN

Visiting Hannibal, Missouri, birthplace of Samuel Clemens/Mark Twain, was on my bucket list. I was so excited when I finally got there.

Hannibal and the Mark Twain Boyhood Home and Museum did not disappoint. I took my time going through the Interpretive Center and Museum and the historical buildings. Seeing the homes of the people that inspired Becky Thatcher and Huck Finn, and walking the streets that Twain himself walked, thrilled me to no end. It felt like I was inside the books. After seeing the town, I made my way to the dock to take the steamboat cruise along the Mississippi. The hour-long cruise was lovely and the captain narrated along the way, pointing out special spots and offering facts about the river, the boat, and the land-marks along the banks.

As an author, I love visiting the homes of famous writ-ers. A few years later, I visited Twain's home in Hartford, Connecticut. It's quite grand, but I didn't get the same feeling of connection that I did when visiting Hannibal,

Missouri. Shortly after that, I wrote a piece for Winneba-GoLife on the authors' homes of New England and included Twain's Hartford home in the piece. I also did a piece on the homes of Southern writers.

On my way to visit my friends, Bill and Sharon, in Marble Hill, Missouri, I took a detour to the small town of Chester, Illinois. Chester was the hometown of Elzie Crisler Segar, the creator of Popeye. To honor their favorite son, the town has erected statues of the characters from the Popeye comics. As you enter Chester, you are greeted by Popeye himself at the Visitors' Center. I got a map of the location of the statues and visited many. There is also a Popeye Museum, but when I was there it was closed. It was a very fun detour.

Finally, I made it to Bill and Sharon's place. I spent a couple of days there. They live on a huge piece of property in the country, and it was so peaceful. Bill and Sharon are both writers, and while there, I had a book signing at a store where Sharon sold antiques. They also took me on a tour of Cape Girardeau and treated me to lunch at Lambert's Restaurant. Lambert's is known for their huge yeast rolls, which they throw at their guests. The food was very good and the thrown rolls were, too. Yes, I caught one.

I had another book signing not too long after that in Kentucky. Along my route was the town of Metropolis, Illinois, the hometown of Superman. Or, at least, his hometown as stated in the comics. In front of the courthouse is a huge statue of the superhero. The town square is also called Superman Square. This town has really gone overboard with all the Superman stuff. Across from the statue is a Superman museum. A little ways up the road, heading back to the highway, there was a bronze statue of Lois Lane that is almost life-size. It was another fun stop.

I love visiting quirky, fun stops like Chester and Metropolis. I discover them all the time in my travels.

23

PRODUCTIVE PET-SITTING IN ILLINOIS

I stayed a couple of nights in the Eureka Campground on Lake Barkley in Kentucky before moving on to visit my long-time friend, Susan, in Madisonville. It was a lovely campground. I haven't returned, but would like to one day. While there, I got a lot of writing done. I love writing outside when the weather is good. We had some storms pass through, but there were enough sunny breaks to work outside quite often. While I was there, many other campers who frequent the campground stopped by to say hello. As a rule, most campers are very friendly. As a woman alone, I often find that in small campgrounds the locals keep an eye on me. Not in a creepy way, but they let me know that if I need anything to just ask. It gives me a nice feeling.

Next, I landed in Madisonville. Susan and I have known each other for decades, going back to working together in Southern California. Susan moved to Kentucky when she retired and this would be my first time visiting her there.

After spending time catching up, I moved my van to her

friends Dottie and Steve's place. They have a large, lovely piece of property on a pond and plenty of room for me to park the van. I was in Madisonville a few days, during which I met a lot of Susan's friends, many of whom had Susan and me over for meals. Everyone was so gracious and welcoming.

My presentation and book signing at the local library went very well. Every seat was taken and the conversation and questions were lively. Afterward, several people from the library took us to lunch. Susan took me on a tour of the area the following day, including Owensboro, a cute town which has a wonderful revitalized riverwalk area.

I greatly enjoyed my time in Kentucky. Madisonville is even featured in my novel, *Finding Zelda*.

From there, I drove north to Batavia, Illinois, for my next pet-sitting assignment. Batavia is west of Chicago. It was a six-hour drive, but I divided it up into two days. My charges this time would be a feisty little terrier named Peyton and two cats, Gracie and Jimmy. I was scheduled to be at this home for two weeks. When I got there, I met the owner, Charlotte, and her son. I liked them instantly. The son was going to college in the DC area and his mother was driving him there. They left the morning after I arrived. This was my favorite pet assignment. The cats weren't very social, but easy care. Peyton was a hoot. He also had a penchant for peeing in the house, so I made sure we took three walks a day, especially one before bedtime. I got a lot of exercise during those two weeks. Peyton would march in front of me, his little ears flapping in time with his peppy gait. At night, he would watch TV with me. He stayed near me while I wrote and became my fun little companion.

During my time in Batavia, I did a lot of writing and

even finished *Finding Zelda*. After doing daily chores, I would sit at the kitchen table and write for hours. I started a new article for WinnebaGoLife and even edited a draft of an audiobook. There was something about the place that sparked my motivation. Maybe it was the on and off rainy weather, the animals, or the comfortable house, but I was on fire creatively.

While in Batavia, I also got some errands done, like a haircut and other small stuff. I checked out the town, which was very nice. In my second week, Bill, a member of my extended family, dropped by on his way across the country on his motorcycle. We went out to dinner and he stayed the night. I would miss seeing him when I finally got to Massachusetts, so I was happy he contacted me for a visit.

One of the best things that occurred in Batavia was a lunch I had with a long-time reader who lived nearby. Jessica is also a graphic designer, and I had used her to design my new bookmarks when I first went on the road. Although I had a book cover designer, I asked her about designing the new covers for my Odelia Grey series. I would be getting the rights back soon and would need new covers. I liked the old covers, but often felt they didn't capture Odelia or the story very well. I also couldn't use them on the reprints. Jessica tossed out ideas for the new Odelia look and I loved them. She also saw my vision for the cover for *Finding Zelda*. She now does all of my covers for books I publish independently.

Not only was I productive in Batavia, but I had some decisions to make regarding a new and unusual series I had percolating in my brain. I asked Jessica about it and polled some of my writer friends. In the end, I decided to go ahead with my idea for a series about a young woman hiding in plain sight from her past while living on the road in a travel trailer. Originally, the series was going to be called Girl Off The Grid, but it is now my *Dead Woman Driving* serial novel series. I love writing this series and am currently working on the tenth episode.

24

THE ROAD TO FAMILY

From Illinois, I started making a beeline to Massachusetts toward my family. My first overnight stop was in Elkhart, Indiana, at the RV/MH Hall of Fame, which is a Harvest Hosts location. I have stayed in this location a couple of times when zipping across the country. It's a great spot for an overnight stay. This is also known as the RV Museum. The MH in the name refers to mobile homes, not motorhomes as one might think.

The next morning, I visited the museum. It was a fun place with a very cool exhibit of recreational vehicles from as far back as 1913. Who knew that RVs and travel trailers went that far back in history? I loved seeing all the different trailers and RVs from over the years. They even had a "house car" owned by Mae West that dates back to 1931. She used it to go back and forth to movie sets. There was also a trailer used by Charles Lindberg.

As I walked through the museum, I got the idea of doing a piece on it for WinnebaGoLife, so I asked if I could speak to the head of the museum. I was in luck because the president was in his office that day. He gave me a lot of wonderful history and information. That night, I proposed the idea to WinnebaGoLife and they loved it.

My next stop was the United States side of Niagara Falls. I didn't have a valid passport at the time so couldn't see it from the Canadian side. Still, it was very impressive. It was a cool, damp day and during the week so there weren't many people around. Since then, I've visited the Canadian side of Niagara Falls, which I found even more spectacular.

From the Falls, I continued driving, stopping that night at a truck stop. It was raining, and was supposed to rain most of the next day as well. It was a six-hour drive from the truck stop to my family in Massachusetts. That's way more than I like to drive in one day, but I decided to do it. I took off early the next morning in the rain and was eating dinner with them that evening. In the previous chapter on weather, I talked about being visited by an officer in the rain while using my bathroom during this drive.

This was my first visit to see my family in a long time. It's wonderful visiting when you bring along your own bedroom and bathroom. The van was parked in front of their large garage, which made it very easy for me to come and go, as well as pop into the house to visit.

I stayed a month, breaking up the visit with short trips. I took a two-day trip to Vermont to see my friend, Stacia. Another two-day trip to Cape Cod. And a trip to Haverhill, Massachusetts, where I was born. The reason for this last trip was to visit an uncle who was ill with cancer, as well as cousins I hadn't seen in a very long time. This last little trip was the last time I saw my uncle, as well as an aunt who came to the gathering.

I had been to Cape Cod before, but it was many years ago. During this trip, I drove to the very tip of Racer's Point, which is a national park. It was a beautiful drive. On the way back, I spent a night at Nickerson's State Park.

Another overnight trip was to see friends, Linda and Tom, who live in Connecticut. They also own a Travato. I had a great time with them talking about travel and our vans. I spent the night in their driveway. Halfway between their house and my family's place is a restaurant called Traveler Food and Books. I had never been before, so I stopped for lunch. It's a fun café with a used bookstore. When you buy a meal, you can choose up to three used books to take with you. Now, I try to get there every time I visit Massachusetts. I enjoy their food and supporting a local business that loves books. After lunch, I went out into the parking lot to find a couple checking out my van. We chatted and it turned out they were friends of Marlaine, my sister-in-law. Small world!

The month went by quickly. I wrote, visited, got back in tune with my family, and enjoyed being in New England. I return for a lengthy visit every year now. It's wonderful seeing the kids in our family grow and being able to experience some of their events in person, like birthday parties and graduations. Almost every week, my sister-in-law goes to a coffee chat group. Originally, they met at the local Dunkin' Donuts and called themselves the Dunkin' Divas. Now, they meet at a local senior center. I so look forward to seeing these lovely people when I visit, and many have become good friends. I've also tagged along on semi-weekly trivia dinner nights with other friends who have now become my friends. Even though I'm originally from Massachusetts, I've never lived in the Brookfield area. Yet, it's become home.

During my first visit to see my family, I did a presentation at their local library. It was to their book club and they had read my first novel, *Too Big To Miss*. It went very well and some of my family attended. A few years later, I did a presentation at the West Brookfield Senior Center about my travels.

Before I left Massachusetts that first year, I visited Cape Cod again, this time with the Winnie Bs. There was a meet-up at Coastal Acres Campground in Provincetown. Originally, I hadn't planned on attending, and it was booked up. But when some spots opened, I decided to go. I spent three nights camping with my friends there and had a great time. It was a lovely way to cap off my trip to Massachusetts.

25

VIRGINIA IS FOR FRIENDS

After I left Massachusetts, I headed down the coast. I had a very busy calendar during the last quarter of my first year. There were a lot of library events on the horizon, as well as visits with friends.

Along the way, I stopped at the Pez Visitor Center, which is really a Pez museum. This was such a great stop on a rainy day. Most of us had Pez dispensers as kids, and many collected the different ones. It's not that large of a place, but it's filled with all of the dispensers made throughout the years and tells the history behind the company. It's also part of the Pez factory and you can watch them making the candy through glass windows. There are also many collectibles and dispensers and candies for sale. If you're near Orange, Connecticut, do consider dropping into this fun place.

Speaking of candy, I also stopped in Hershey, Pennsylvania. I wanted to do the historical trolley tour but it was sold out for the entire day. Tip: Do not try to visit Hershey on a weekend. Instead, I settled on just taking in Hershey World. It has a ride that takes you through the chocolate making process, then dumps you out in the middle of the largest candy store imaginable. Of course, I bought a few things, but my favorite thing was the giant s'more available in the food court. This is a serious s'more that they make upon request with huge graham crackers and marshmallows they make themselves. You even get to choose which flavor of Hershey bar you want them to use. It was so big and decadent, and I enjoyed every messy bite.

Touring Gettysburg was on my bucket list. I camped near it for two days hoping the rain would stop enough to go. I could have gone to the museum, but I also wanted to do the driving tour of the battlefields. I ended up shelving that visit for another time. Several years later, I did finally visit Gettysburg. It's an amazing place. If you haven't been there, go. When you go, get the audio for the driving tour. Like most historical places we learned about in school, nothing compares to seeing the locations in person.

Next up was Virginia. I stayed with my friends, Janet and Alan, my first few days in Virginia. Alan Orloff is another writer and we had so much fun talking about the business of writing, both the pros and cons. After that, I stayed with my friends, Janet and Chris. I have a lot of friends in Virginia, and it was so nice mixing visits with library events.

My first library event in Virginia was in Annandale. Janet and Alan came, and so did Janet and Chris. I had a wonderful surprise when Karen, one of my Travato friends, dropped by, too. I only knew her from online up until that night. The event was very successful.

My next library event was in Winchester, Virginia, at the Handley Library. The Handley Library is one of the most beautiful and stately libraries I've ever seen. While in Winchester, I stayed with my friend, Ann. Her apartment complex gave me permission to park a couple of nights at the end of their large parking lot. Perfect! We had a delightful visit and the library event was another success. Some online friends came to that, too, so I got to meet them in person.

Before I got to Winchester, I had a few extra days to tour. I decided to drive the Skyline Drive in Shenandoah National Park. I entered the park north of the southern entrance. At the gate was a sign announcing that all campgrounds were full, but the ranger told me I might find some last-minute openings. I drove along Skyline toward the north entrance, stopping to drink in the beauty and take photos. Fall was here and the trees were ablaze with color. When I got to Mathews Arm Campground, the sign said it was full, but the ranger there said I could put my name on a waiting list for any spots that might come open due to cancellations or people leaving the first-come-first-served sites. This campground had both first-come-first-served and reserved sites, but they wouldn't know if they had anything open until checkout time. I put my name on the list, then pulled over to wait and see. Even though the waiting list was long, I snagged a site for a couple of nights. I really enjoyed my few days in Mathews Arm Campground. It's snuggled in the woods and so peaceful. It didn't have hookups, but with my van that wasn't an issue. I took a lot of walks and got a lot of writing done. A few years later, I traveled the entire length of Skyline Drive, north to south, and stayed at a different campground near the south end.

Often, I get asked if any of my travels get put into my novels. Yes! You can look for Mathews Arm Campground and Skyline Drive in my upcoming *Zelda Doubles Down*, the second Zelda Bowen novel. Other travel adventures are also great additions to my fiction. Many show up in my *Dead Woman Driving* episodes.

On my bucket list was Thomas Jefferson's Monticello. The plan was to see it after I left Winchester. Unfortunately, the day I was in the area we received more rain. Not just sprinkles, but big rain. The next day, it was nice out. I was able to visit Colonial Williamsburg after spending the night at a nearby Cracker Barrel.

I really enjoyed Colonial Williamsburg. It was another of those historic sites that makes history that was so dry in school come alive. I walked all over the place, going in and out of buildings, taking photos, listening to the guides, and drinking in the history of a place that was occupied by both the British and American armies at different times. When I go to these types of places, I like to sit on a bench and absorb the atmosphere until I can almost see the colonists and soldiers walking the streets as they once did.

After Williamsburg, I drove to Belle Isle, Virginia, where I met up with more Winnie Bs at a campground. I was there several days, enjoying the good company. Everywhere I went in Virginia, it was beautiful, whether I was in a campground, on backroads, or even in more urban areas. I enjoy traveling through it every time I do.

26

HEADING SOUTH

I had always wanted to see the wild horses of Assateague Island in Maryland, so I decided to make that happen. Before leaving Belle Isle, I made reservations at the Assateague Island National Seashore Campground. One of my favorite things during the drive there was crossing the Chesapeake Bay Bridge-Tunnel. This consists of three sections of bridge and two very long tunnels. The entire thing is seventeen miles long. It's truly an amazing feat of engineering.

I spent the night at the large rest area at the end of the bridge. This is a great place to stay whether you need a place before or after traveling the bridge. The next day, I checked into my campground at Assateague. And there were horses! Lots of them! They were on the road leading to the campground. In the campground. Along the beach. Everywhere.

I spent several days at Assateague Island National Seashore Campground. After a few days, I drove into the nearby town to do laundry and run some errands. But mostly I stayed at my campsite, writing and watching the wild horses wander in and out of the campground. One day, I was at my picnic table writing when one decided to visit me. I quickly gathered up my computer and went inside my van. There are rules in the campground to not get within forty feet of the animals, but the horses never got that memo. They will approach, hoping for food. They will kick and bite if they feel threatened. Once, I watched a horse barrel through a campground with several tents. It knocked over pots and tables until a man shooed it away. These horses are beautiful, but they are wild, and should be respected as such. Just like bison.

After leaving Assateague, I spent two days driving leisurely down the coast to meet up with friends, Scott and Crystal, at the Cabela's in Raleigh, North Carolina. They own a Travato, and Scott is a mobile repair guy. I asked them to meet me so Scott could check my van's batteries, which were still wonky off and on. He did find a loose wire and fixed it. He also checked my solar panels and battened them down tighter. Over the years, Scott's done a lot of repair work on my van's electrical system, including installing new batteries a few years later. While we were there, another Travato couple dropped by and we had a great visit.

A few days later, I was in South Carolina visiting my friends, Mary and Tom. I couldn't driveway surf at their home because of HOA rules, but after my visit I drove a little bit down the road to a Cracker Barrel. The night before, I was at a Walmart. See, I do sleep around.

In two days, I had a library event in Carolina Shores, North Carolina. I left the Cracker Barrel early in the morning and went to a rest area north of the library to work. I stayed there until it was time for me to head to the library to meet Christi, the librarian, and one of the library patrons for dinner. It was a lovely day, although a bit breezy, and the trees were gold and red. I sat at one of the picnic tables and worked. I also reflected on my life as a nomad. I'd promised myself that I would take stock of my new life after a year and decide whether or not I wanted to continue. My year would be up in two months. It was becoming very clear to me at this point that I would be staying on the road.

After dinner, Christi brought me back to the library. I had been given permission to spend the night in their large parking lot. An interesting note, Christi is now a nomad herself! She travels all over doing the most interesting seasonal work-camping jobs. I visited her a few years later at Glacier National Park where she was driving a shuttle bus for the summer.

The next day, I worked from my van until it was time for the library event. It was very well-attended and we had a lively discussion about my work and travels. I could've stayed another night in the library parking lot, but opted instead to start moving north toward Springfield, Virginia. I'd agreed to another pet-sitting job there, even though it was backtracking. That night, I ran into a wicked storm right after I settled in at a Cracker Barrel for the night. I'd called my friend, Janet (yes, another Janet), who lived in the area, and the next morning I met her for breakfast at the Cracker Barrel. In the past, I only met up with her when she came to California to see her son. It was nice to be able to visit with her on her turf for a change.

The next day, I had to check in for my pet-sitting job, so after breakfast I drove until I was barely over an hour from there. This was peanut and cotton country. I stopped and bought some delicious peanuts. The cotton was already harvested, but bits of it were scattered all over the road and stuck in fences. It looked like the field had dandruff. I stayed in a rest area in Virginia for the night. The next morning, I got a call from the people I would be pet-sitting for over the next week. They were going to a party that afternoon and would let me know when they were home. This gave me a lot of time to kill, so I found a park near them and settled in for some work and relaxation.

Lake Accotink Park was large and beautiful with many walking paths, a large lake, picturesque train trestle, and a reservoir waterfall. Even the drive from the main road to the park was gorgeous. The road was canopied and lined with brilliant fall foliage. Once at the park, I put on some walking shoes and started walking around part of the lake, taking photos and enjoying the lovely, crisp fall day.

My charges this time were a bouncy miniature Australian Shepherd named Sofie and a cat named Tiger that stayed mostly outside. I found it so funny that often when I walked Sofie, Tiger would follow. The cat would never get close to us, but she was always there. I walked Sofie several times a day and often played ball with her. She was sweet and had so much energy. She was wearing me out, but in a good way. One day, Tiger even brought me a gift of a dead mouse. Such love!

After reading one of my Facebook posts about my location, I received a message from a cousin named Wanda. I'd never met her, but knew of her. It turned out that she lived just a few miles from where I was pet-sitting, so I went to her house for coffee one afternoon. We hit it off right away and still stay in touch.

The pet-sitting gig went smooth and easy. It was a nice house, nice people, and sweet animals, but I decided that I would put pet-sitting on hold for a bit. My schedule was getting pretty booked into early next year. Of course, at this time, I had no way of knowing how much everyone's schedule would change in 2020.

From Springfield, I went to Lewes, Delaware, to see my friend, Chrys, a Travato owner and wonderful painter who was doing a presentation on her art. Other Travato friends, Bernie and Marcia, were going to be there, too. I made a reservation to stay at the same campground as Bernie and Marcia near the event. It was cold and rainy the couple days we were there. It got below freezing the night before we left and was still barely above freezing when I took off from the campground. On the way out, I dumped my waste tanks in freezing temperatures with flakes of snow whirling around me, but I needed to do it. Believe me, I did not dawdle.

Chrys's presentation was wonderful. After, I started heading south with plans to stay the night at the rest area just before the Chesapeake Bay Bridge-Tunnel. I took a lovely scenic route that took me near Assateague. Along the way, there were fields dusted with snow. It may have been fall, but winter was definitely coming.

My next destination was Brookgreen Gardens in South Carolina, which came highly recommended by several friends. Beyond that, I didn't have any plans until Thanksgiving, when I would be visiting my cousin, Judy, and her family in Florida. I decided before I left the rest area to meander south on smaller routes, also recommended by friends, and take my time. I found a small, inexpensive campground in Windsor, North Carolina, that had full hookups and called them to make sure they had openings. They did, so I made that my destination for the day.

Along the way to Windsor, I stopped at Dismal Swamp State Park. I walked around the canal area and took some photos, but it was cold and windy, so I didn't venture far. In spite of its name, Dismal Swamp State Park is quite beautiful, even in the cold.

Cashie River Campground in the small town of Windsor, North Carolina, was a great find. There weren't many RVs or trailers there, so I got my pick of spots. It had a nice bathhouse and even laundry facilities. I registered for two nights, but ended up staying five because of some big storms heading up the coast. I rode them out at this nice little campground before heading on my journey again. I barely left my van during those days, until the last day after the storms passed. My days were spent hunkered down and writing.

One afternoon, my neighbors, Carolyn and Patrick, invited me over for tea. They were also waiting out the storms before moving on and were very nice. Carolyn was from Scotland, so I was treated to a proper tea with Earl Grey tea and scones with lemon curd and jam.

I finally made it to Brookgreen Gardens. The place was stunning! Built by a man named Huntington for his wife, a sculptor, it's a huge collection of gorgeous ponds, reflecting pools, gardens, and sculptures. There is also a Low Country exhibit, along with animals of the Low Country in a zoo format. I spent hours there strolling through the gardens. Everything is beautifully maintained. Each Christmas, there's an annual event called Nights of a Thousand Candles, and they were getting ready for it. Throughout the park, there were hundreds of candle pedestals installed and luminaries ready to go. In the ponds, glass bowls floated that would later contain candles. There were tents and chairs and tables ready to be set up for the initial night's reception. I understand this is a spectacular event. Some of the lights were already installed in trees and behind sculptures. Even in the daylight, when the shadows fell, you could see them and tell how beautiful it was going to be.

I spent that night in a Walmart just outside of Charleston, but the next day I decided not to see Charleston this trip. Instead, I made reservations for two nights at Fort McAllister State Park in Georgia. I loved this campground. The park has a lot of historical sites to see and paths to walk. I settled in and enjoyed my time, often spending it outside walking or writing at my picnic table. I enjoyed it so much that I booked two more nights.

On my third day, I drove into Savannah. I'd never been there before and really enjoyed it. It's a crowded, historical city, so I parked my van in the parking lot for the Old Savannah Trolley and grabbed one of their hop-on-hop-off trolleys. I took the trolley all the way around the city before deciding to hop off near the Riverwalk for lunch and some sightseeing. Later, I grabbed it again and got off at Forsyth Park. I explored this area with its gorgeous homes, including the Mercer-Williams House used in the book and movie, *Midnight in the Garden of Good and Evil*. I would love to return to Savannah someday. There's so much to see. But I still need to see Charleston.

27

MORE FAMILY AND FLORIDA

I had not seen my cousin, Judy, and her family in many years, so it was enjoyable to spend Thanksgiving with them. Judy and her husband, Jack, lived in Palm Coast, Florida, in a beautiful home right on the Intercoastal Waterway. Also there for Thanksgiving was Jack's brother, Bud. Judy and I walked their dog and had long talks about our families, especially memories we had growing up. Her father and mine were brothers and very close, and our two families spent a lot of time together. At Thanksgiving, I got to meet her grandchildren. It was a wonderful visit. Sadly, Jack passed away a while after that, so I was very glad I got to visit them.

A few weeks later, I visited my Aunt Pauline and Uncle Len, who also lived in Florida. Pauline was my mother's last surviving sibling. It was great visiting them, too. As sad as it is, being so mobile has enabled me to visit long-time friends and family before their passing. Sometimes, I was aware that they would soon be gone. Other times, their deaths were surprising. I guess it's both sad and happy at the same time.

Except for flying in and out of Florida to catch a cruise ship and once to visit Disney World, I'd never spent much time in the state. There were two Florida items on my bucket list that I checked off during this visit. One was going to Key West and seeing Ernest Hemingway's home, and the other was visiting the home of Marjorie Kinnan Rawlings. As I mentioned, I love visiting the homes of famous writers. After leaving my cousins, I drove down the coastal highway for a few days, taking my time.

I stopped at the historic lighthouse at Ponce de Leon Inlet and visited Manatee Lagoon. I didn't know much about manatees, except that they were large, gentle sea creatures. The visitors' center was very informative and there was a balcony where you could look for the animals. I was in luck the day of my visit. There were a few manatees in the small lagoon, including a very young one.

My next destination was Marathon in the Keys. A former Travato owner managed a marina and restaurant there and offered me a free place to stay in my van for a few days. What a gift! RV parks and campgrounds in the Keys can be super expensive, especially the closer you get to Key West. And no matter the cost, they are very difficult to get into and often fill up six months in advance. The marina turned out to be a great place to write and relax, and the weather was perfect.

The day after arriving at Marathon, I took off for Key West. The drive was really interesting. Highway 1 was mostly a narrow two-lane highway going over bridges and through small seaside towns. It links all the various keys together, ending with Key West. It was a warm, lovely day and the water was unbelievably gorgeous. Some of the keys I passed through were tiny, and some of the towns were barely more than a few stores. I drove from Marathon over the Seven Mile Bridge and into keys with names like Little Torch Key, Big Pine Key, Cudjoe Key, Bahia Honda Key, Upper Sugarloaf Key, and Lower Sugarloaf Key.

When I arrived in Key West, I found parking in an all-day lot close to the Sloppy Joe's restaurant where I was meeting Travato friends for lunch. It was so great to see Jim and Rhonda again. The last time was at the meet-up at Fort Flagler in Washington. It's so wonderful how you can meet someone in Washington State, one of the most northern points in the U.S., and have lunch with them in Key West, the most southern point, just a few months later.

After lunch, I visited the Truman Little White House. This was President Truman's summer home and it's quite beautiful. On the same street down a ways was the Hemingway House, the top priority on my sightseeing list. I loved the Hemingway House. Besides the house tour, I spent a lot of time poking around all the nooks and crannies of the property. The large pool was interesting because at the time it was built, it was quite an undertaking, and in the 1930s, it was the only in-ground swimming pool within one hundred miles. While on the tour, a young man proposed to his girlfriend right in front of everyone. She accepted and the people in the room went wild with delight.

There were many of the famous six-toed cats milling about, oblivious to the strangers coming and going. Most were sleeping in the sun, as cats do. Behind the house was an extensive cat kennel with wooden houses and perches where the animals can be kept safe at night. There were also small houses scattered around so they could get out of the sun or have privacy during the day. Also behind the house was a cat cemetery in a small tree-lined alcove with markers for each animal that had passed. It nearly made me cry to think that I was walking in the same steps as Hemingway, or standing at the edge of his pool, or looking at his kitchen. Ernest Hemingway lived here. He wrote here.

From there, I headed to the iconic southern most point of the United States, a sea buoy at the end of Whitehouse Street. The line to take your photo in front of the buoy was long, so I just snapped a photo with other people in it. Then, I walked a block to the free shuttle stop and took it back to the parking lot and my van. I had to get moving because I was meeting Peggy, another Travato friend, for dinner back in Marathon. By the way, I didn't discover that they had a free shuttle service around Key West until after I had walked miles.

Two days after leaving Marathon, I was in the northern part of the Everglades. The road was bordered on both sides by a canal, swamp, and various waterways. When I turned into Everglades National Park, I was greeted by two Everglades residents, a giant blue heron and an alligator. Both were on the side of the road enjoying the sunshine. Once inside the park, I made my way to the Shark Valley Visitor Center. I wanted to take the tram tour, which was highly recommended.

The tour was over two hours long, amazing, and very informative. Along the way, the ranger accompanying us told us everything about the park, including history, vegetation, animal life, and conservation efforts. We saw many alligators in the wild, mostly sunning themselves. We even saw a couple of clusters of baby alligators with their momma nearby. Alligators were everywhere. The tram stopped at most of those next to the road so we could take photos. Beautiful birds were also everywhere. We saw great blue herons, small blue herons, great egrets, wood storks, vultures, and kites among them.

One of the things that surprised me was how the area was mostly grassy marshes. There were tree islands and lots of cypress trees, but mostly it was marsh grass for miles and miles. A sea of grass, it was called. There were also many ponds and pools. Although we didn't see any, we were told the area was also home to bears, cougars, and white-tailed deer, as well as the invasive python.

Just over halfway along the tram tour, there is a concrete observation tower with a wide, mildly pitched ramp that goes up to the observation deck. There is a higher area accessed by a steep spiral staircase, but that area was only for ranger use. From the observation deck, you could see for miles across the Everglades. It was stunning. There was a river down below, and while we were there a huge turtle swam by. Many large alligators clustered around the base of the tower near the water. There was even a crocodile in the mix. The ranger said this particular crocodile comes every year to that area.

The alligators rule here. They are often on the roads and walkways. One was near the path to the tower, and some stupid people got close to it, even though the ranger gave them several warnings. It reminded me of the fools who get close to the bison out west.

After the tour, I stopped at the Big Cypress Gallery, which features the incredible photography of Clyde Butcher. He is considered the modern Ansel Adams. I bought a couple of Christmas gifts, some cards, and a T-shirt featuring his photograph of a ghost lily, which I saw in the Everglades.

I was spending the next three days at the Midway

Campground. This campground is set up really well. The campground forms a large oval around a pond. The road and a day-use area are between the campsites and the pond. The pond contains alligators and there are signs everywhere not to feed or approach them, or swim in the water. There was even a sign warning people not to walk their pets near the water's edge.

I was only set up for a short time and settled in to read when I heard my name being called. I looked out my slider to see a man getting out of an SUV. He called out his name and I recognized him from Facebook. Marty is a former police officer and writer who follows me online, but we had never met. He was camping up the road and figured out where I might be from my Facebook posts earlier in the day. He stopped by to say hello and meet me in person. We had a wonderful time talking and laughing. Marty is a born storyteller. He and I are now great friends and have met up several times on the road over the years.

Midway Campground was a good place to stay for a few days, except for the weak connectivity. I got a lot of writing done, did a lot of walking around the loop, plus I completed some little fixes around the van. After three nights, I was relaxed and ready for the road again. On my last full day there, Peggy, whom I had last seen in Marathon Key, showed up. She and her friend were just staying the night. The three of us visited at a picnic table and another camper came by and joined us.

A couple of days later, I checked into Silver Springs Campground in Ocala. This was another lovely campground. While there, I was going to speak at their library. Plus, I wanted to visit the home of Marjorie Kinnan Rawlings since it was not very far away. My friend, Sue, was going to be camping there, too. She used to live in Ocala and was instrumental in getting me the speaking engagement.

The day after I checked into Silver Springs Campground, Sue, some of her friends, and I went to Silver Springs to take the glass bottom boat tour on the Silver River. This used to be an amusement park, but when that failed, the state turned it into a state park. The glass bottom boat tour and our guide were a lot of fun. This area of the river is fed by many natural springs, and the water is fresh and clean and replenished constantly by the springs. In addition, this area was used to make many TV shows and movies over the years. Shows like Sea Hunt, I Spy, some Bond movies, Tarzan movies, and The Creature From The Black Lagoon were made here.

The bottom of the springs is filled with caves and caverns, as well as remnants of canoes and ships left by the Spaniards and Seminoles. Along the coastline of the river live tons of turtles and birds and other Florida wildlife. Supposedly, during the making of the Tarzan movies, there were some monkeys left behind that populated the area surrounding the river. We didn't see any monkeys, but we did share the river with dozens of kayakers.

The next day was my last library event of the year. It was held at the Freedom Branch Library in Ocala. Afterwards, they told me it was one of the largest turnouts and best presentations they'd had. Even my friend, Marty, showed up. More and more these days, people seemed more interested in my travels than my books, but they bought books, too. Later, I had cocktails with a group from the Friends of the Library at one of their homes, then went out to dinner. It was a long but very lovely day.

The next day, I visited with Sue at her campsite and extended my reservation at Silver Springs by one more day.

Being December, I was lucky they had a spot for me. I was getting tired of all the running around. I had been on the go for a long time and it was catching up with me. So, I made reservations for one week at East Bank Campground in Georgia, and the following week at Davis Bayou Campground in Mississippi. Both came highly recommended.

Since I had to move my van to a new spot for the one night I extended my stay, I used the time between checking out and re-checking in to drive to Cross Creek. This was the tiny town where Marjorie Kinnan Rawlings lived while writing *The Yearling* and other books.

The drive to Cross Creek was very peaceful and interesting. I drove along a small highway through horse country and passed some amazing horse farms. I even passed Jumbo-Lair, a gated community with the longest private runway in the United States. Each home has access to the runway, hangars, etc. I also went through some lush marsh and swamp areas, and areas with much more modest homes. It was raining in the morning when I got up, but slowed to just light rain as I drove. By the time I got to my destination, the rain had stopped, though still threatening.

Marjorie Kinnan Rawlings State Park is a small park with picnic tables and a playground. To the right of the parking lot is access to the Rawlings home and farmland, which is a national historic site. Unfortunately, I got there just after one of the tours had begun and the next was not for another hour or more. Instead, I did the self-guided tour, but that didn't give me access to the inside of the house. It was still a lovely place to visit. As with the Hemingway home, it gave me chills and not just a little bit of excitement and inspiration to be walking the same ground as a Pulitzer Prize winning author.

After leaving the Rawlings home, I went down the road

to have lunch at a restaurant called The Yearling. The food was very good and they have a gallery of photos and memorabilia from the making of the movie *Cross Creek*, a movie I love and have seen a few times. I had my first gator bites here, and the first grits that I liked. In fact, I loved them. Another culinary surprise was their sour orange pie.

28

THE END OF MY FIRST YEAR

East Bank Campground is on Lake Seminole, just over the Georgia and Florida border. I had a great campsite right on the lake. Although I haven't had a chance to return, it remains one of my favorite campgrounds.

Shortly after I settled in, I spied another Travato a few sites over. I knew Becky and Robert from the Travato group, but had never met them before. We became friends and they had me over for dinner. We visited off and on during my stay.

It rained quite a lot while I was at East Bank. I spent the rainy days writing up a storm. In fact, it was there that I began writing this book. I tend to work on several projects at once. Besides working on this book, I was working on a new novel and a short story. In between rainstorms, I would take walks. It was a very productive week.

I was leaving East Bank on my birthday. The day before, I dumped trash and took a walk. I stopped by Becky and Robert's campsite to say goodbye. There was a great egret that hung out by the culvert next to my campsite and I found it amusing. I mentioned it to Becky and Robert a few times. The night before I left, Becky presented me with a birthday card with a lovely drawing of the egret that she had made. Becky named the egret Eloise. Eloise still hangs in a place of honor in my van many years later.

The next day, my sixty-seventh birthday, I drove many hours, often through heavy rain, to get to Davis Bayou Campground in Ocean Springs, Mississippi. I arrived too early to check in, so I went to the non-smoking casino in Biloxi. My father always said one should gamble on their birthday, even if it's just buying a lottery ticket. When I left to check in at the campground, I had almost two hundred dollars in winnings. Happy Birthday to me!

It rained all that night. The next day, it stopped but was very cloudy. I decided to run some errands before more rain came in. My first stop was the dock and beach in Ocean Springs. The last time I was there was about ten months earlier. I had sat on the dock looking out over Biloxi Bay and was overcome with emotion. I had done it! I was on the road full-time. How did I get so lucky to have this life? Now a seasoned van-dweller, I wanted to sit on that same dock and see if I felt the same emotions. Unfortunately, because of all the heavy rain, the area around the beach and dock was flooded, even the parking area. The sky was gun metal gray and the air wet and cold. I looked out at the dock, instead of slogging to it. The feeling, though, was still the same. I still felt deep gratitude that this was my life.

From the beach, I went to French Kiss Pastries and bought a couple of their tiny cakes for a belated birthday celebration. I also bought some small quiches and scones. Then, I headed to the grocery store to buy things for a nice Christmas dinner before returning to camp.

Here's the thing about Christmas—most of my adult life, I have celebrated Christmas alone. And that's okay, so please don't feel sorry for me. I am a family of one, and that's not something I declare to put on a brave face. I am a family of one, and I am not lonely, except for fleeting moments. From childhood until early adulthood, Christmas meant family fights and people getting drunk. Over the years, I would often go to other people's homes when invited, but that didn't always feel right, either. Depending on the people, I often felt like a stray they took in. A holiday charity case. For the past twenty-five years, I have mostly celebrated alone, making myself a nice dinner and enjoying the peace and quiet. Sometimes, I share that meal with others.

Maybe this is why I am so well-suited to nomadic life.

Christmas Eve Day was lovely. I opened up the van and aired it out while I wrote at the picnic table. I also brought out my butane camp stove and cooked a nice meal. After being mostly cooped up because of the weather, it was grand to spend so much time outside.

Christmas Day, I was restless. I worked in the morning on a short story that wasn't coming together. The more I worked, the more disjointed it became. I talked to my family in Massachusetts and other friends. I decided not to cook a nice dinner, but to go out. The restaurant I wanted to go to was not open, so I went back to the casino and had dinner there. I gambled, but broke even. Which is really a win, isn't it? Finally, I returned to the campground. I tried working on the short story some more, but the more I did, the more I knew something was off with it and my frustration grew.

The next day, my writing started coming together. I wrote like a crazy woman from early morning until early afternoon. I was on fire, working the kinks out of the story. Later, this short story would become the first episode in my *Dead Woman Driving* serial novel. In the early afternoon, I received a message from Sandy and Robbie, more Travato friends. They were in the area and asked if I was up for a visit. When they left, I got out my grill and made a great dinner of salmon and asparagus, celebrating Christmas a day late.

On the one-year anniversary of my retirement from my paralegal job in Los Angeles, I found myself in Louisiana at Bayou Teche Brewery. It was a Harvest Hosts location where I planned on spending the night. The day turned out to include a couple of firsts. On the way to the brewery, I stopped and got some cracklings and boudin to try. I didn't care for the boudin but enjoyed the cracklings.

After settling in at Bayou Teche Brewery, I took a tour of the brewery and ordered a flight of beers. I enjoyed my beers outside where they had tables and chairs set up. The place had live music on Saturday afternoons and people were arriving for it. They also ran a pizza place on those days. At the brewery was a restored Airstream trailer outfitted as a cigar lounge. It was beautiful inside with wood paneling, a humidor cabinet, and leather sofas. I visited it with one of the women at my table who wanted a cigar. Later, I went back and had my first cigar. John, the man who owns and runs the cigar lounge, picked out a mild one for me. I sat outside and smoked it right down. It started to rain lightly, but I stayed outside. I didn't want to move near the people eating at the café. Inside the trailer, it was smoky from others smoking. The rain started and stopped. Near the end of my cigar, it started raining harder. I stayed outside, finished the cigar, and got thoroughly soaked. But what a time! All during this, the band was playing Zydeco music and people were dancing and eating. Whole families were there, enjoying the music and dancing. It was fabulous. One of my favorite things was watching a man dance with his very young daughter, who sported butterfly wings. It was definitely a place where people come often, even driving many miles to get there.

After I finished my cigar, I was a bit wobbly. Not sick, but a bit buzzed. I went to the café and ordered a Killer Tomato pizza and handmade root beer. I quickly ate two pieces and started feeling better. When the band finished, I went back to my van and settled in. A bit later, the place hosted music trivia. The music was loud, but it ended by nine. I slept like the dead that night, but in the morning I had a headache and a horrible taste in my mouth that took a couple of days to go away. That was my first and last cigar, but it was fun and a grand way to celebrate a full year of retirement.

The next day, I visited the Tabasco Factory on Avery Island, Louisiana. There's a museum and a self-guided tour of the factory and grounds. During the tour, I learned about peppers, the famous sauce, and how it's made. I was there on a Sunday, so the factory was not running, but I was able to see it. I had lunch at the on-site café where they served Creole food. I ordered crawfish étouffée and maque choux, both delicious.

From there, I drove to the Jungle Gardens, which was started by the founder of Tabasco. It's a preserve of special plants, lagoons, and wildlife. You can drive, walk, or bike the three-mile road. I drove it, but my van was too tall to do one part of the loop. At that section, they have RV/Bus parking and you can walk the short loop trail in that area. The weather was looking pretty sketchy, so I drove on, bypassing that section. The gardens were impressive, especially the massive oaks and timber bamboo.

I spent the last two days of 2019 at Rainbow's End, the Escapees RV Park in Livingston, Texas, and where I get my mail. There was a lot of mail waiting for me, including Christmas gifts. I used those days to do chores and clean up the van. I was also writing up a storm again.

On December 31, 2019, one year after I began my life as a nomadic writer, I was holed up in my van writing this travel book. My fingers danced across the keyboard as I listened to the fireworks outside. When I went to bed, I reflected on the past year. I had promised myself one year and I had made it. And it was a hellava year!

SECTION THREE

A PANDEMIC COMES KNOCKING

"Where shall I go? What shall I do?"
— **Scarlett O'Hara in Gone With the Wind**

30

SHELTERING IN PLACE

Originally, this book was only going to be about my first year of being a nomad and the time leading up to that life-changing decision. But when 2020, my second year living on the road, got turned on its head, I knew I'd have to address this as well. It changed everything, as it did for many people.

I first started hearing about COVID-19 when I was camping in Quartzsite, Arizona, with friends. It was in the news, but just as something that might happen, not the killing boogeyman it turned out to be. I left my friends in January for another speaking engagement. This one was a large fundraiser event in Southern California. I was the keynote speaker and they had booked me a year in advance. I was so excited. My speech was very well-received and I sold every book I had with me. It was a big success for them and for me. Little did I know at the time that it would be my last speaking event for nearly two years.

Following the event, I visited with friends in Southern California, then headed back to Arizona to spend more time with my camping friends. When a few of us traveled back into the San Diego area for a meet-up, I was not feeling well. Shortly after I arrived at the campground, I felt worse and decided to go to an ER about an hour away. My friend, Stacy, came with me. I was diagnosed with diverticulitis. While there, we heard some talk about the COVID virus, but it was played down. When we returned to our meet-up, a few people were concerned that we might have brought it back with us after being in the ER. Fortunately, we had not.

After the meet-up, Stacy and I returned to Quartzsite and camped with other friends. We were there until late March when things started closing down for the season. It was about that time that everyone was being told to go home and shelter in place to avoid the virus. This was when everything started shutting down. When you're a nomad, the road is your home. And they were talking about sheltering for several months. Where would I do that? Should I return to Texas, which was now my domicile? If I decided to find a place in Arizona, would I be welcome, or would they demand that I go to Texas?

I confess that I started to panic. Not about the virus, but about where to go in such a situation. Some states were already closing their borders to out-of-state travelers. Doors were being shut everywhere. Stacy decided to return to her home in South Dakota. I decided to travel with her until we got to Texas, then I would decide what to do. Friends who were camping in National Parks were sent packing, actually being asked to leave so the parks could close down. Some state parks were evicting out-of-state visitors, or also closing down. A few friends found monthly rentals in RV parks. I checked out a few of those and found that some of them were price gouging in the face of the emergency. Many RV parks closed their doors to campers only wanting a few days or a week. If you couldn't commit to and pay upfront for two or three months, they didn't want your business. My options were diminishing daily. Some friends even opted to do short-term leases on apartments. Others, like me, took their chances on the road.

By the time I returned to Texas, I had hit upon an idea of how to "shelter in place" cheaply. Texas, especially the western part of the huge state, has a lot of community RV parks where campers can stay anywhere from one to five days for free or for a small donation. These RV parks often have electricity, water, and even dump stations. Some are very nice. Others, not so much. I made a list of them and started making the rounds. I did find a few closed because of COVID, but most stayed open. Plus, in Texas, you can stay overnight in rest areas. Although many of the bigger rest areas—the ones with facilities—were closed, small pull-outs and picnic areas without facilities were still open.

For a couple of months, I bounced from town to town, from rest area to rest area, parking lot to parking lot, staying as long as I was allowed before moving on. I wore a mask everywhere and picked up my grocery orders in store parking lots. My travels made an odd-shaped circle around the area as I revisited towns and dug in again for a few days. I got to know a lot of these small towns quite well. During this time, I met another nomad doing the same thing. We kept running into each other at these small-town RV parks, and we exchanged information on new sites as we found them. Eventually, we moved from town to town together. It certainly made sheltering easier to have a buddy going through the same thing. It became our own little bubble.

By the end of May and into early June, some states were opening up. There were still some that were not, but I was itching to leave Texas. It was also starting to warm up, and soon the Texas summer heat would arrive. As soon as I could, I left Texas and started north toward cooler temperatures. I kept track of which states were now allowing out-of-state travelers. Some allowed it openly, while others allowed it with mandated quarantines for new arrivals. I avoided the ones with quarantine requirements. Even if a state was open to travelers, many state parks were still closed to out-of-state visitors.

While traveling, I kept to myself and continued to look for small-town RV parks. I found many in the Midwest. My friend left Texas soon after I did and we met up in the Dakotas. Together, we toured North and South Dakota, mostly staying in parking lots, city campgrounds, or other campgrounds as they opened up. We kept to ourselves, as we did in Texas. When he had to return to Texas for a family matter, I continued my travels through the Midwest. When the Army Corps of Engineers campgrounds started opening, I stayed there for two weeks at a time, which was the maximum time allowed. With my senior National Parks pass, they were fifty percent off and a real bargain. I found most of the free campsites and town RV parks on the AllStays, Campendium, and iOverlander apps.

Most museums and other attractions were still closed in 2020, but outside venues were opening. Most attractions that were open required the wearing of a mask. I still managed to see a lot of very cool things while keeping away from most people. It took planning and research, but I managed to shelter in place and later travel using common sense.

Winnebago's Grand National Rally for 2020 was canceled, as were other meet-ups. I crossed those off my calendar. In 2020, I knew I wouldn't be visiting my family in Massachusetts, either. Speaking engagements disappeared. All the plans I'd made for 2020 were now gone. It never occurred to me to leave life on the road behind. I was determined to adapt.

As the summer wore on and turned to fall, things began to loosen up even more. I continued wearing masks in public places. In some states, I was mocked for wearing one, but I didn't give in to the pressure. Most of my travel entailed staying in campgrounds for a couple of weeks at a time, then moving to another. I found myself enjoying this change of pace after spending 2019 buzzing around the country. I spent more time outside and got a lot of writing done. I felt fortunate that while others were often stuck inside with limited travel and personal contact, I could take my home with me and continue with my work. It was definitely less confining than what most people were experiencing.

To my knowledge, I never got COVID, but even years later, I still avoid crowded places.

31

THE MOXINATOR

In 2020, many people adopted pandemic pets. I was among those who did. It really helped with the loneliness of being restricted. My friend, Jess Lourey, a noted novelist, loves to foster kittens for a local shelter. In August, she'd found homes for all three kittens of one young momma cat, but no one wanted the momma. I took one look at that sweet feline face and contacted Jess. If she could keep that kitty just a week or two longer, I would drive to Minneapolis and adopt her. Jess happily consented. I filled out the shelter paper-work online. On August 19, 2020, I arrived at Jess's home and took possession of a small, black female cat. Her foster name was Monica, but I immediately changed it to Moxie, after the New England soft drink. She is definitely full of moxie, and has been my heart's delight ever since.

People will tell you that you should slowly acclimate a cat to travel. Poor Moxie had none of that luxury. Jess passed her off to me in a carrier I supplied and off we went. I had already outfitted the van with a litter box, a cat bed, food dishes, and a couple of toys. I drove to a campground just over the Wisconsin border and settled there for several days in order for Moxie and me to get used to each other. We bonded very quickly. She wasn't the first cat I'd adopted, but she was definitely the easiest to get to know. Or maybe she had a bit of Stockholm syndrome. Whatever it was, by the end of our camping in Wisconsin, she was sleeping with me on my bed. It took a while before she would let me rub her belly, but slowly she trusted me enough. Now, she begs for belly rubs on a daily basis.

As explained previously, Moxie still dislikes the driving part of being a van cat, but she loves the camping part, even if it is just an overnight stop. She is a nosey little thing and will watch our camping neighbors with great interest, especially if there are children and dogs around. But her favorite thing is to watch the birds and squirrels.

A week after adopting Moxie, I decided to train her to walk on a leash. We were in a campground in Minnesota. I put the little scamp in a harness, attached the leash, and took her outside. In under five seconds, I was holding a leash with an empty harness on the end. Moxie ran around the campground, going from my campsite to others, exploring and sniffing. I tried to catch her, but she would duck under other rigs or scamper out of my reach. I called to her. I tried to entice her with treats. She slipped past me and went down into a shrub-covered ravine where I couldn't follow.

My heart sank. One week in and I'd lost my cat. She'd run away. No matter how cozy we'd gotten, it had only been a week. I was sure I'd seen the last of her. I returned to my campsite, sat at my picnic table, and cried. Soon, I heard a meow. There she was, out of the ravine and near the van, looking at me. I slowly tried to get close, but she took off again. I sat back down and watched her as she traveled around the campground exploring. I would call her name and shake the treat bag and she would come back, but not let me near her. I sat and waited, hoping she would return before the predicted rain began. Soon, she returned to the van and came close to me, but when I tried to grab her, she took off. She did that several times before I realized she thought it was a game. She was playing and teasing me. Eventually, she got tired of the game and I snagged her and got her back in the van. I was relieved and so happy that in a very short time Moxie had come to understand that the van and I meant home and security.

About a week after that, Moxie earned her keep by catching a mouse that had the misfortune of invading the van. It hadn't happened before and hasn't happened since. I was camping in Ely, Minnesota, in a field that belonged to an RV park. I'd gone to Ely to visit the International Wolf Center and the North American Bear Center. Both of these places were excellent, and I highly recommend visiting them.

The excitement began when Moxie woke me up in the night with loud crying. At first, I thought something was wrong with her, especially after seeing spots of blood on the floor. I picked Moxie up and examined her, but found no wounds or cuts. She wiggled to be let go. Then, I saw a big field mouse on the floor, and it was moving slowly. Moxie leaped from my arms and went after it, smacking and terrorizing it while I watched in horror. She chased it in that confined space until it disappeared somewhere near the front. I didn't see where, but I could only assume it went out the way it had come in. At least, I didn't find a rodent body or smell one later. My friend, Stacy, has tagged Moxie the Moxinator for good reason.

Moxie is quite the hunter. She's fascinated by squirrels, chipmunks, birds, and about anything else that moves

outside. It has led to her escaping the van a few times. I have
a large screen door on my van's sliding door. When I first
got Moxie, she was content to look out through it at the
outside world. One day she got out, and since then she's
determined to have her own adventures. I blocked and
barricaded the screen door at the bottom when the sliding
door was open, but in time she figured out how to get past
the barricade. She is smarter than I am.

A few times when she's gotten out, friends have
captured her, since I can't chase her with my gimpy knee. A
couple of times, she's gotten out when I couldn't retrieve
her. Those times, she has come back to the van in her own
good time. The first time she got through the screen door,
she was going after a ground squirrel at GNR at the
Winnebago Fairgrounds. I was writing at my desk and she
was on the ottoman watching one of them through the
screen. She launched herself at the screen, and it popped
outward. Off she went like a shot. She didn't go far, but
spent quite a bit of time under one rig or another until my
friend, Jonne, crawled under one and grabbed her.

Once, we were camping at Lake O' the Pines, one of my
favorite campgrounds in Texas. I had the sliding door open,
but well barricaded so it would not pop open.

Or so I thought.

I had just finished washing dishes and turned around to
see what Moxie was doing. I couldn't find her. I glanced out
the screen door. There she was, wandering our campground, yet the barricade didn't look disturbed. She had
simply pushed against the screen until it gave enough for
her flexible body to squeeze through the bottom beyond the
barricade. I went outside to the picnic table. She did her
scampering away thing, so I wrote while she explored. As
much as I worry about her, I can't chase her. My knees are

not up to it and it makes her run faster and farther away. About an hour later, she returned to the van but wouldn't let me grab her, not even when I put out treats. I went inside and did a few things. A little later, she was at the screen, asking to come in. I opened it and she hopped inside, done with her adventures for the day.

I did not adopt dumb.

You might ask why not let her roam since she knows where home is and she returns. But I often camp in places where there are lots of critters. I don't want Moxie to become lunch for a coyote, hawk, or eagle, or any other wild thing.

From time to time, I take her outside in her carrier, which is expandable. Moxie loves going out to the picnic table and being outside while I write or do chores near her. When expanded, the carrier is quite large with a lot of space for her to stretch out and watch the world. She's still not allowing any leash training. I have a new harness that she cannot escape from, but whenever I take her outside with it, she has a meltdown. Still, I continue to try.

32

THE PORK TENDERLOIN TRAIL

One of the few things I give 2020 credit for is helping me to become more creative when it comes to finding things to do in my travels. Normally, I visit my family in Massachusetts in September for a few weeks, but in 2020, that was impossible. Instead, I did a tour of Iowa, including taking on the Iowa Pork Producers Association's Pork Tenderloin Trail.

The Pork Tenderloin Trail is a collection of restaurants that have what is considered some of the best pork tenderloin sandwiches in the state. There were about twelve or so restaurants listed. At the first one you visit, you get a card. Once you have a pork tenderloin sandwich at ten of the restaurants and receive a stamp from each, you mail the card into the Iowa Pork Producers Association and they send you a T-shirt. Pork tenderloin sandwiches are a thing in much of the Midwest, but in Iowa they take it very seriously. It's a pork cutlet, pounded until it's thin, then battered or breaded, and deep fried. They're usually served on a bun that is way too small for them. Think of the meat as wearing a small hat and you'll have a pretty accurate picture. They are delicious, but they are generally quite large. I quickly learned to use the bun as a template. I would cut around it to make a normal size sandwich, then take the rest of the meat back to the van for leftovers.

I had my first pork tenderloin sandwich at the Belmond Drive-In just down the road from the Winnebago Visitors' Center, where I spent a couple of nights. The next one was that same day at Gramma's Kitchen in Walcott, Iowa, across from the World's Largest Truckstop, where I spent that night. Both sandwiches were delicious, although different. As I ate them, I started taking notes, thinking this might be a good article for WinnebaGoLife.

In between the two sandwiches, I visited the Field of Dreams movie site in Dyersville. The ballfield from the movie is still there and well-maintained, along with the farmhouse. There are bats and balls to use, and the man at the gate told me that a lot of people leave old ball mitts and balls in tribute. I sat on the bleachers and enjoyed the day as I watched families play catch on the famous ballfield. Some tried their hand at hitting balls, aiming for the cornfield. It was a lovely way to spend time in the sun and fresh air.

The World's Largest Truckstop along I-80 is amazing. I spent the night there that night, and another night a few years later. There is a section for RVs that is out of the way of the trucks that file through the place. I didn't mind the noise because I can sleep most anywhere now, but it was Moxie's first truck stop and it was a doozy for her first time. There was so much noise and movement outside that she was on sensory overload and wouldn't calm down for the longest time. I had my blinds down, but only used my privacy curtain across the front instead of my big shades, which I usually do when only spending a night somewhere. Moxie spent most of the night up in the cab area, wide-eyed, bouncing between fright and excitement, and often waking me up. By the next time we stayed there, Moxie was an old hand at truck stops, and she did great.

The third pork tenderloin sandwich took me to Clinton, Iowa, to Stouts Irish Pub, and from there to tour the Sawmill Museum in the same town. I was actually on my way to meet a friend at a campground in Wisconsin, and this town was not far off my route. Three sandwiches down, seven to go. As I said, these sandwiches are often huge. After the third one, I had a lot of leftovers in my van's fridge.

On the way to the campground in Wisconsin, I went through the historic town of Galena, Illinois, and stopped at the home of Ulysses S. Grant. I missed the tour, so I visited the lovely park by his home. Then, it was off to Potosi, Wisconsin, and an evening at a brewery that was a Harvest Hosts location. It was quiet in their parking lot, and both Moxie and I got a good night's sleep.

Although my campground was just a few miles from the brewery, it was way too early to check in, so I made a big round trip to another restaurant to try another pork tenderloin sandwich. This restaurant was historical and only open Friday, Saturday, and Sunday. It was Friday and I would be camping the rest of the weekend, so off I went. Breitbach's Country Dining was located in Balltown, an Iowa town of about sixty people. The restaurant was founded in 1852 and has been in the family most of that time. It is said that Jesse James—the outlaw, not the biker—dined here.

Their pork tenderloin sandwich was one of my favorites overall. The owner came over and chatted with me a bit. They were closed much of 2020 because of COVID, and were slowly opening up again. All the food was delicious, including the pie, which his wife makes herself every day.

This place might have been out of my way, but it was a true gem.

I finally checked into my campground in Wisconsin and met up with my friend, who was camping there with another friend of hers. I was there for several days before getting back on the Iowa Pork Tenderloin Trail again. It was a nice break for both me and my stomach.

Back in Iowa, I did some minor sightseeing until I reached the next pork tenderloin sandwich on my list, which was at Goldie's Ice Cream Shoppe in Prairie City. This was one of my favorite sandwiches. It was takeout only when I was there, but they had picnic tables.

That night, I spent the night at La Vida Loca Winery, a Harvest Hosts location. I was sitting outside talking with the owner when he asked if I was going to visit the Bridges of Madison County. *What? Where?* I loved that book and the movie. It turned out that I was in Madison County and didn't realize it. I immediately changed my plans for the next day. One of the great things about not having a hard-set plan is that you can zig instead of zag.

The next morning, I set off to see all of the Bridges of Madison County. I had a great time doing that. I found a map of them online and went to every one, often driving miles over rough farm roads to get to them. One of the bridges was in Winterset, the birthplace of John Wayne, where there is also a John Wayne Museum.

In Corning, about forty minutes away, was another restaurant on the Pork Tenderloin Trail. The sandwich at Three C's was very good. It was also just blocks from the birthplace of Johnny Carson. I drove by his home, but it was closed.

Instead of going back the most direct way on the highway, I decided to head north on smaller roads. My next stop was an interesting one. It was the site of the first train robbery in the west, which was executed by Jesse James. There was a nicely designed pull-off on the road commemorating the place. On display was the piece of original railroad track that Jesse James removed in order to stop the train.

Several miles up the road was the small town of Stuart, where I continued my crime scene tour. This was the location of the First National Bank robbed by Bonnie and Clyde. A few more miles up the road was Dexter, Iowa. In Dexter is Dexfield Park, where Bonnie and Clyde's gang shot it out with the police in 1933. The Barrow gang was rounded up and arrested at this location, while Bonnie and Clyde got away. This is an overgrown area, not a regular park.

After spending the night in a casino parking lot in Des Moines, I was ready to check another sandwich off my list. I ate at the Brick Street Market in Bondurant. Dinner time found me eating another sandwich, this time at the Lucky Pig Pub and Grill in Ogden, Iowa. Eight down, two to go!

My ninth pork tenderloin sandwich was at a place called Dairy Sweet in Dunlap. By now, I was craving anything but pork, but I pushed on. Twenty minutes away was the small town of Elk Horn and Larsen's Pub. I figured I would take the sandwich from Larsen's to go and have it later for dinner. However, when I got there, the restaurant was closed and a note said they wouldn't be open again for five days. *Five days!* There was another restaurant on the Pork Tenderloin Trail I could have gone to, but it would have meant backtracking many miles. I had gone by this one a few days earlier and also found it closed with limited hours when open.

The next morning, I decided I didn't want to backtrack

and needed some time off the road to catch up on stuff. I waited out the reopening of Larsen's Pub at a county campground in Atlantic. It was a nice little spot, and I enjoyed being there and eating something other than pork.

Finally, it was time to polish off my last pork tenderloin sandwich. The restaurant wasn't going to be open until suppertime, so I visited the towns of Elk Horn and Kimballton. Together, these two rural towns are known as the Danish Villages. Kimballton has a charming park of sculptures centered around the stories of Hans Christian Andersen. The center of the park is The Little Mermaid fountain. Elk Horn has the oldest working windmill in the United States. It was built in Denmark in 1848, then brought to Elk Horn and rebuilt in 1975. Also on the grounds is a Viking smithy shop and home and a chapel built in 1951 by Danish immigrants. It was a charming display on lovely grounds.

By the time I saw everything, it was time to head to Larsen's Pub and take on my last pork tenderloin sandwich. The dining room was not open because of COVID, and they didn't have any outside dining. It was strictly a takeout window at the time of my visit. So, I took my food and went to a small park to eat.

I was done. I had eaten all ten sandwiches required by the Pork Tenderloin Trail. As much as I enjoyed the food, it was a long time before I ate pork again. In the process, I saw a great deal of Iowa. Who knew that eating pork tenderloin sandwiches could lead to visiting famous bridges, birthplaces of American icons, movie locations, and crime scenes?

A few months later, I finished writing the article on my accomplishment and sent it to WinnebaGoLife. They loved it and promptly published it. The Iowa Pork Producers

Association even contacted me about using the article, which they eventually did. I sent in my card with all ten sandwich stamps and the Iowa Pork Producers Association sent me a very nice T-shirt. I never wore it, though. You see, on the back in big letters was #IowaPork. No woman, especially a large one, wants that on her back.

33

WE'RE NOT IN KANSAS ANYMORE

I spent the rest of September 2020 visiting attractions and staying in small-town campgrounds in Kansas. One of my favorites was Marysville, Kansas. They have a few spots in their city park. I spent several days there, waiting out thunderstorms and visiting the town. It's a cute town and was a major stop for the Pony Express. The Pony Express Museum was closed because of COVID, but I returned a couple of years later to see it. It's a wonderful museum, and you should see it if you're in that area.

Marysville is also known for its black squirrels, both real and statues. The city park is filled with black squirrels. Around the town are black squirrel statues painted in colorful garb to represent the company or place in front of which they stand. There is even a small historical site at the park. While staying at the Marysville park for the first time, I was treated to a rehearsal of the town's high school marching band.

Alma, Kansas, is another great little city park with hookups. I spent a few days there cleaning my van thoroughly on the inside. There are only three or four sites, and they charge a very small fee. I've stayed there a few times over the years, but the last time I went by, it looked like people were using it long-term and there were no sites available. I was so disappointed.

Between Marysville and Alma, I visited the town of Wamego, the location of the Oz Museum. This is an excellent museum, especially if you love the books of Frank L. Baum and the movies based on them. On the outside, the museum doesn't look that large, but inside it's quite extensive and covers not only all things Oz related, but the life of Baum. There was also a really cool collection displaying copies of all of his books, not just the Oz books. I had no idea how prolific he was, or how ground-breaking in many ways and in many areas. He even had his own film company and produced silent films. Halfway through the museum is a small theater where the movie *The Wizard of Oz* with Judy Garland plays on a loop. They show the entire movie, not just clips. I got there just as Dorothy was captured by the Wicked Witch and stayed until the credits.

Kansas was certainly not lacking in interesting museums. After Alma, I drove to Topeka to visit the Evel Knievel Museum, which is housed in a local Harley Davidson store. The museum is fascinating, even if you aren't into motorcycles or daredevil tricks. I remember watching Knievel on TV when I was young. The museum contains many of his motorcycles, memorabilia, his tour bus, outfits, and his complete history. I really enjoyed it.

The next stop in Kansas still remains as one of my favorite museums ever. Strataca, located in Hutchinson, is also a Harvest Hosts location. I tried to visit Strataca earlier, but it was closed because of COVID. Now, it was open and I was eager to see it. I reached there late afternoon and spent the night. The next morning, I was on the first tour of the day.

This was, hands down, one of the best and most informative tours I've ever taken. It took at least two hours. Part of it is self-guided, and the rest of it contains guides and rides. It started with me being given a hard hat, followed by a ninety-second ride in a large elevator six hundred fifty feet underground in the dark. Not a single light. This was not a tour for anyone afraid of the dark or enclosed spaces.

After a brief intro, I was left in a huge hall, all carved out of rock, where I could read about the formation of the salt deposits millions of years ago and other history. At the end of the hall, I entered another huge area and was greeted by a woman who gave me the information on the museum and how best to enjoy it. To my left was another large hall. This one contained displays of equipment once used in the early days of the mine. There were short videos spaced throughout, talking about the process then and today and the equipment used. At the end of this hall, I turned right and was greeted by the guide who was going to do the train ride portion of the tour.

I boarded a train with wooden seats with the guide sitting in front driving the engine. It reminded me of rides at Disneyland. A recorded explanation of each display was played whenever we stopped. The ride was dimly lit, but at each display it was automatically highlighted. I learned about the life of the miners underground and the process of mining. Most of this part of the tour focused on the extracting and removing of the salt from the mine on a rail system, now replaced with something more modern. The small railway we were traveling on was built from the rails of the old rail system. When the train returned to the starting place, I entered another self-guided display. This

one was about the storage facility in the mine. *Color me
surprised!* There are forty-five acres of storage in the mine in
which important documents, information, and many original movies and movie memorabilia are stored to keep them
from being destroyed by time. The mine temperature is
consistent and it's dry.

Next, I was greeted by another guide who would take
me through the Dark Ride portion of the tour. I boarded a
large cart and off we went into another part of the old mine.
I learned that there are three separate companies that
operate in the mine: the museum, the storage company, and
the salt mine. I also learned that the salt mined in this
particular mine is used primarily for road salt.

This part of the tour focused on how the miners cut
out large halls with massive pillars as they extract the salt,
including the type of machinery used. Basically, the walls
are cut, then the salt extracted by blasting. Machines
broke up the salt into smaller chunks with employees
filling carts. Years ago, the men who filled the carts were
paid in brass tokens, a token for each load they filled. The
tokens were turned into the paymaster for their pay. It
took a man one and a half hours to fill a cart and the
tokens were worth fifty cents each. Most men made about
two dollars a day. This was during the 1930s. Today, the
salt is mined with fewer people and with more technology,
but the salt walls are still cut and blasted. One of the
videos I watched focused on employees working in the
mine today.

At one point, the guide turned off his head lamp and we
were in total darkness. You couldn't see your hand in front
of your face. He discussed air circulation and safety.
Machinery and vehicles used in the mine are fueled by electricity or by diesel to avoid dangerous emissions. It was an

amazing amount of information. This is definitely a museum that should not be missed.

From there, my road led me to Wichita. I viewed the Keeper of the Plains statue there, which is magnificent, and also the Cowtown Museum. Set alongside the Arkansas River and the legendary Chisholm Trail, Cowtown is a large living history museum with historical buildings and artifacts depicting life in Wichita from 1865 to 1880.

34

SADNESS IN OKLAHOMA

On my way from Kansas to Texas, I went through Oklahoma. I didn't have a lot of time before I needed to be back in Texas, but there were two things I wanted to see in Oklahoma City. One was the Oklahoma National Memorial and Museum, which memorializes the 1995 Oklahoma City bombing, and the other was a very large sculpture installation memorializing the 1889 Oklahoma Land Run.

I arrived on a Sunday, which was perfect because trying to get downtown to the bombing memorial would have been a nightmare during the week. There wasn't much parking down there for my van and there was a lot of road construction. Being Sunday, I was able to park in the post office parking lot across the street from the memorial.

The first thing I noticed was a statue on the corner on the property of Saint Joseph Catholic Church across from where the bombing took place. The statue is called *And Jesus Wept*. At the time of the bombing, a parish house was standing on that spot. It was so severely damaged that it had to be torn down, so the church erected this beautiful memorial in its place.

The next thing you notice as you cross the street to the memorial and museum is the fence with all the memorial items attached to it. There are T-shirts, plastic flowers, photos of victims, and notes from loved ones. It was extremely moving. And I thought, if this fence is making me cry, what is the museum going to do?

The Oklahoma National Memorial and Museum is very well laid out. It contains three floors. After you enter and pay the admission, you are directed to an elevator that takes you to the second floor. The exhibit begins there, depicting events of the seemingly normal morning. At the time the bombing occurred, the Water District Board was having a meeting in the building in which the museum is now located. The sounds of the bombing were caught on the audio recording that was being made of the meeting at the time. You go into the meeting room and they shut the doors. In semi darkness, they play the audio for you. It's disturbing, to say the least. You listen to a common board meeting with common discussions for a couple of minutes, then the bomb, the screaming, and the chaos is clearly heard.

The rest of the museum is dedicated to the bombing, news media coverage, rescue and recovery efforts, and the aftermath. Throughout, there are videos playing with different aspects of the day and the days that followed. There are also computer terminals that you can click on to hear stories of the survivors. There was one video near the end of the second-floor exhibit that talked about the volunteers who came from all over to help Oklahoma City.

The next floor was mostly dedicated to those who were killed in the bombing. One hundred sixty-eight people were killed that day, both adults and children. As some of you may recall, there was a daycare center located in the building that was destroyed. There is a gallery of the victims' photos and names. The photos are set in individual Lucite boxes, and inside the box are items that were important to that individual.

Finally, you go back down to the lobby and outside to visit the memorial park where the Murrah building once stood. It's a beautiful park, the centerpiece of which is a long, lovely reflecting pool. The reflecting pool is bordered by two arches. To the right of the reflecting pool are one hundred sixty-eight small sculpted chairs representing the victims. The whole thing was moving and heartbreaking. I'm so glad I took the time to see it. I spent many days after that visit thinking about it. I remember the day when the bombing happened, but seeing the museum and memorial really brought it home, even many years later.

In my travels, I have visited many tragic and sad sites and museums. The Flight 93 National Memorial in Pennsylvania, which I saw a couple of years later, was one site that left me sad for days. On September 11, 2001, Flight 93 was hijacked and rerouted to collide with the U.S. Capitol. The passengers and crew overcame the hijackers and the plane crashed in a Pennsylvania field, killing all on board, but sparing the Capitol. The crash site and museum are well worth a visit to remember these American heroes and the ultimate sacrifices they made that day.

I was also moved for days after visiting The Legacy Museum and The National Memorial for Peace and Justice in Montgomery, which are dedicated to the history and victims of slavery and racism. These are other sites that I believe everyone should visit and which leave a lasting impression.

So, why are these types of museums and memorials important to visit? Why make a point of seeing these places of sadness, instead of only seeing and doing fun stuff? Because they're an important part of our history and a stark reminder of the evil people can inflict upon others. Maybe if we're reminded of this, we'll be able to be much kinder to each other. At least, that is my hope.

After visiting the Oklahoma bombing memorial, I drove about ten minutes through downtown to the river to see the memorial to the land run. This very large, bronze sculpture installation was stunning and impressive. It's considered one of the world's largest bronze sculptures and contains forty-five figures. There are wagons, horses, and people, even a man on a bicycle, all in a frozen frenzy as they rush forward to claim land in this historic giveaway. The park it is in is lovely. I spent quite a bit of time walking around and snapping photos of the different bronze figures. There was even one on the far end of a man standing next to his horse, ready to plant his flag on his new land. The detail of these bronze figures is incredible.

35

ITCHY WHEELS

On and off during the latter part of 2020, friends of my friend, Larry, contacted me about house-sitting for them while they spent the winter in the Southwest. They lived in Tumwater, Washington, just outside of Olympia. I wasn't too keen on doing house-sitting again, especially in the winter, and they were vacillating about going because of the surge in COVID during the last quarter of the year. In October, they decided they did want to go to Arizona and contacted me. By now, with COVID on the rise again, I agreed, especially since they had a heated garage in which I could store my van for the winter. I like the state of Washington, and it would give me a safe place to stay during the COVID surge. It would be a different kind of sheltering in place.

I spent the last few weeks of October and early November in Texas, taking care of my van's inspection and registration and voting. I also visited several friends in the state and met up with friends at campgrounds. Then, Moxie and I set off for Washington. Along the way, I visited with some friends in New Mexico and Utah. I also took in some attractions in Idaho, like the Museum of Clean and the Idaho Potato Museum. I was also writing up a storm on a couple of projects along the way. Mostly, I was focused on getting to Washington before it got cold.

Once I arrived, I spent a few days with the owners, getting instructions and learning about the house before they left and I moved in. They had two small birds in a large cage to look after. I was surprised that Moxie didn't bother with them much. Often, she'd sit on the table across from the cage and watch them for a long time, but she was more interested in the birds at the outside feeders. The house had great floor-to-ceiling windows and a big desk in front of those in the front of the house. I spent many hours writing there while Moxie watched the birds. I even got out my binoculars and learned to identify many of them.

It was during this last house-sitting job that I encountered the syndrome I tagged as itchy wheels. I was there for four months. The first month, I settled in and was fine. The second month was good, too. I got a lot of writing done and thoroughly cleaned up the van and updated it. I got into a routine of writing in the morning and working on the van in the afternoon. I ordered a lot of things I needed since I had an address for delivery, including new sturdy shades for the windows. I had the use of their car to run errands, which made it much easier to do shopping.

My van developed some electrical issues, and one of my Travato friends who lived in Washington came up and repaired it with phone assistance from other owners. Another Travato friend visited during my stay. Larry came by and stayed a couple of days in his van. While in Washington, I was able to renew my passport and even got my first and second COVID vaccinations. Near the end of my stay, as COVID restrictions continued to relax, I got my first haircut in almost a year and met up with a friend from college who lived in Seattle. We visited the Chihuly Garden and Glass Museum together. I discovered a local casino and won some money. It even snowed while I was there. So, those four months were very productive and enjoyable, as well as providing a semi-shelter.

But as the days and weeks went by, I found myself slipping back into my old habits of eating too much and watching too much TV. I tried to get more walking in, but the cold would go right through my achy knees. In spite of having a lot to do, and the reopening of things, I got listless and bored. By the time the owners returned and I left Washington, both Moxie and I were more than ready to get on the road. I thought Moxie would whine when I returned her to the van, but she surprised me and seemed as eager as I was to embrace our home on wheels again.

Itchy wheels. That's what I call it, even now. I still get it when I sit too long in one place, even when I stay with my family. I'm okay for a couple of weeks, but any more than that and I start falling into old bad habits and get antsy for the road. This may sound silly, but I start feeling confined and it makes me nervous.

SECTION FOUR

FINDING MY LONG-TERM RHYTHM

"Not all those who wander are lost."

— J.R.R. Tolkien

36

A FLUID LIFESTYLE

With my first year spent getting used to my new life and the second year spent dealing with the uncertainty of a pandemic, by my third year, I found myself getting into a rhythm. I was settling into a nomadic lifestyle that suited me. Nesting, you might say, but my nest had wheels. Unlike my previous stationary lifestyle, my life on the road was ever-evolving, but it still had a steady rhythm.

The year or so spent dealing with the pandemic taught me to be more aware of my changing needs. It also showed me how much I enjoyed being still from time to time. Not for long, but in short week-or-two chunks at a favorite campground, usually with a killer view of a lake or river. When I get the urge to nest for a short period, I settle into a nice campground with electric and water hookups and set up my house. I use that time to clean the van thoroughly, to make minor repairs, to write more, to rest more, and to get to know the local community. If there are several nice campgrounds in the area, I might even stay a month, moving from one to another when my allowed time is up at one. Usually, campgrounds allow fourteen-day stays within a month. You can break up those days or lump them together. I prefer to lump them together. It gives me a sense of stability, but not so much as to be confining.

There are certain campgrounds that I return to often, or annually, depending on the weather. I affectionately call East Totten Trail in North Dakota my summer home. Once in a while, I might miss a summer stay there, but not often. Davis Bayou Campground in Mississippi has been my holiday home for several years. Magnolia Ridge Campground in Texas between Jasper and Livingston is my go-to when I need to do things in Livingston, my home base. Along the way, I have collected other campgrounds that I add to my list of favorites and return to when given the opportunity. Instead of sitting in one location, like a house or an apartment, my home comes with wheels, affording me with ever-changing views. If I want to move, I simply drive to a new location.

Years ago, I would never have dreamed that this would become my preferred way to live. But here I am, happier than ever with my living situation. But, remember, it's not for everyone. Some people need the security of roots. I need the fluidity of the road. I believe a lot of people think they want to live as a nomad, but once they experience it, they find it's not for them. Others enjoy it for a number of years, then decide they want to return to a more rooted lifestyle. And that's okay. We all have different needs and likes, and they can be changeable and ever-evolving. We simply need to recognize what suits us personally.

The downside of these longer stays, whether they be in campgrounds or visiting friends and family, is itchy wheels. One winter, I got off the road and bounced for a couple of months between campgrounds in the South that were fairly close to each other. Part of the reason was my propane tank needed to be repaired, so I had to have hookups for heat, cooking, and hot water. I can't dry camp comfortably in the winter without propane, and I was having trouble getting anyone to repair my propane tank during this time. It was eventually repaired months later when I returned to Texas, giving me once again the freedom to roam without needing campgrounds.

That winter, there were two campgrounds that allowed me to stay for a month each. In between, I stayed at others. The plan had been to use the time as a productive writer's retreat. Instead, I became lethargic and unmotivated. At first, I was gung-ho and wrote a lot. I would take walks and use my time effectively. But soon, my productivity and my spirit sagged and I became depressed. I ate too much. Watched too much TV. Played too many video games. Slept way more than I needed. Whenever I talked on the phone with one of my closest friends, I questioned whether or not I should get off the road entirely. I had just turned seventy and felt my life as a nomad was losing its appeal and fun factor. And it was, because I was no longer a nomad. I was once again stationary, although in a van and not a sticks-and-bricks abode. I was returning to the bad habits of my previous life. The lifestyle that had nearly put me in an early grave.

Eventually, I broke out of that quagmire and got back on the road. I started meeting up with friends again. I got my propane fixed. The joy in living a nomadic life returned. I had learned a valuable lesson about myself and my personal needs—I need a balance of travel and camping, of wandering and staying. After that winter, I went back to staying in campgrounds or visiting people for only a week or two at a time, then moving on. It has made all the difference. It is my healthy and happy rhythm.

37

ASSUMPTIONS

Something I thought might be fun to share in this book are the different reactions I get from people who find out I live full-time in a van. When I first set out to be a nomad, the reactions from people I knew ranged from disbelief to awe to envy. Many thought I was nuts. As time went on, I encountered other reactions, including pity.

One particularly long day of driving put me after dark in a Flying J truck stop for the night. I had really pushed myself, driving about eight hours that day. This is something I almost never do, but I wanted to get somewhere sooner than later. A bad heatwave had put me in a campground for an unexpected two days. Now, I needed to make up time to meet up with friends. Along the way, I had stopped for gas and tore a hole in my jean capris on something by the gas pump. Upon arrival at the Flying J, I went inside to buy some windshield washer fluid. While paying, I asked the clerk how much a shower would be. The thought of standing under a shower with unlimited hot water sounded like heaven to me. The clerk looked me over and said, "I'm sorry, dear, but they're twelve dollars." *Huh?* The condescension in her voice was palpable. I knew she meant well, but she'd judged me on how I looked. I kept my twelve dollars.

On the way out, I grabbed dinner at the attached Denny's. I was too tired to make anything for myself. My waitress also looked at me oddly, but she cheerfully rolled with it. After dinner, I made a stop in the ladies' room. No wonder they were giving me looks. Staring back at me in the mirror was a stout, elderly woman with disheveled gray hair, torn pants, a grease smudge on one cheek, and dull eyes with dark bags under them. I was a hot mess. I certainly didn't look like I traveled in a fancy van and was a published author. I looked like I was one step away from a shelter or a ride in an ambulance. Now, I try to grab a look in a mirror before facing the public.

Although the above example is understandable under the circumstances, other reactions are simply based on knee-jerk perceptions. Many women are envious, especially those near my age. Young people tend to think I'm cool for doing this. Trust me, I have not drawn a cool breath in my life. Once, a man dressed in black and riding a motorcycle pulled up next to me, looked the van over, and proclaimed me to be a badass. Ha! But some don't even attempt to hide their judgment.

One woman, upon learning I lived in a van, insisted I needed to "find Jesus." She followed me back to my van from a restaurant, where I'd just had lunch with a friend, determined to thrust Christian literature into my hands. I was as polite as possible, telling her, "No, thank you," repeatedly. When I tried to leave, she blocked my way. Then, I nicely and quietly told her to leave me alone or I would take the pamphlets and burn them. She backed away with her mouth hanging open. As I drove away, she stood on the corner with her family, pointing at me. I know most people would've simply taken the pamphlets and tossed them, but I wanted to make a clear point to her, though I doubt it did any good. But I felt better. She had no idea what my religious leanings were. She never bothered to ask. She equated a life on the road to being a sinful lost soul. This woman wasn't the only person determined to save my soul after learning I traveled full-time in a van.

Then, there are the men I encounter on the road. Most of the men I meet traveling are very nice and respectful, and some have become friends. But every now and then, I meet an old codger who thinks I might be open to his amorous advances. By the way, I can say *old codger* because I am old. These men are generally not full-time nomads, but people who take their Class A rigs or huge trailers to local campgrounds for a week or two, or maybe they travel a month before returning home. Most are widowers and lonely, and I respect and understand that. But whenever I'm in a campground for a week or two, I know that if there is a widower in the campsite, there's a good chance he'll be by to check me out and chat. At one campground, I had three such suitors in the two weeks I was there. I discouraged them all, but nicely. At another campground, a man lectured me on how I should carry a gun, proudly showing me his, never mind that the campground clearly posted no firearms allowed. At yet another, a man said something racist to me. Afterward, he asked me to dinner, as though what he said was nothing more than that the sky was blue. Then, there was the man who declared I must be gay because I didn't accept his advances after several attempts. None of these men have been threatening or angry types. They've simply been clueless. Other women I've met on the road have told me they've experienced the same thing. A woman on the road alone does not mean she is lonely or desperate.

I've also learned that the longer I'm on the road, the more people look in askance at me. At first when I told people I traveled full-time, they thought it was cute, fun, interesting, and/or adventurous. But now when I tell people I've been living in my van for over five years, they often look at me with either pity or apprehension. I think many assume that I'm unstable because I live such an unconventional life at my age. Or maybe they assume I have no other options. One couple I met, who were vacationing in the same campground, offered to find me a place to live. Again, they meant well.

One woman I encountered, who was new to van travel, asked me if I really was happy living this life, or was I putting on a brave face. No, I really prefer this life over one in a stationary location. No brave faces here. In my Novel RV Journal on Patreon, I'm very honest about the times I'm down and doubtful, when my joints hurt, and when I'm frustrated. I don't try to sugar-coat anything. When someone sees me living this lifestyle, I want them to see it for what it is, joys and warts alike. I'm not one of those nomads on the Internet who makes the lifestyle look glossy and glamorous. I particularly laugh at the ones who show themselves scantily clad and draped on their vans without a care in the world. Even those hard-bodied, young van-lifers have to dump their poop, do laundry, fight mosquitoes, and fix mechanical issues. It just doesn't garner them enough clicks and likes to show that.

38
_____

LAST EXIT?

As I finish this book, I'm about to enter my sixth year on the road. When I first started out, I told myself I would give it a year, then evaluate my living situation. The first year came and went. The second year came and went. Then, the third year. A lot of people are shocked that I'm still at it. I'm not. What surprises me is how fast the years have passed.

People often ask if I have an exit plan for getting off the road. Some full-timers will insist that you should have one. I don't have one at all, nor do I feel I need one. I have no end time set. When asked how long I intend to do this, I say, "When I physically cannot do it, or when it stops being fun."

The van is my home, just a home on wheels. Do people who live in sticks-and-bricks homes have an exit plan?

When the time comes for me to turn in my keys and wheels, I'll know it. Or not. Maybe my cold, dead body will be removed from the van after a sudden health episode. I can think of worse ways to pass from this earth.

That said, my family has access to my important information, and I have an up-to-date will and health directive.

I'm not unprepared for the inevitable. I simply plan on staying on the road as long as possible because it's my happy place. I thrive in this lifestyle. So, why upset my personal apple cart?

One thing I've noticed is that as the years have gone by, I seem less compelled to drive all over, staying only a day or two somewhere. Into my third year, as noted previously, I found myself content to stay in campgrounds for a week or more. It's a lifestyle that can easily change. That cannot be said of a stationary home. And how else can I enjoy million-dollar views for zero to fifteen dollars a night? Many times, I've sat at a campsite looking out over a gorgeous lake or bay, knowing I could never have such a variety of stunning views from a stationary home. As I was finishing this book, I spent several nights camped overlooking the Bay of St. Lawrence in Nova Scotia. It cost me nothing. It's a deal that's hard to beat.

How many people can simply up and move if the weather changes? Or clear out if the new neighbors are loud or rowdy? Tired of the view? Pack up the old camp chair and move. Sounds like the perfect exit plan to me.

Maybe I am carny folk.

ACKNOWLEDGMENTS

I have a custom sticker on my desk pedestal in my van. It says: This journey made possible with a lot of help from my friends.

From the beginning of my first thoughts about doing this until now, years later, I have received support from many people in all different ways, from small gifts for the van, places to stay overnight, and major help in repairs and information.

Below are some of the very special people who made this journey possible:

Todd and Shari Swanson, who helped me with the financing of my van.

Stef and James Adinaro of *The Fit RV*, who first showed me that this life was possible.

Stacy Smith, my boon companion and emotional support on many adventures.

Heide van den Akker, my boon companion and emotional support by phone.

Travato Angels, who provided repairs and invaluable information:

Scott Griepentrog
Dan Kamada
Ron Merritt
Greg Schultz
Dan and Faith Seine

All my ride-alongs on *The Novel RV Journal* on Patreon, especially those below:
James Burns
Marge Burglund
Carol Clayton
Chris Hudson and Janet Bradford
Shirley and Doug Pearson
Sandra Wingfield

ABOUT THE AUTHOR

Sue Ann Jaffarian is the critically acclaimed author of three mystery series, various short stories, and novels. In addition to being a writer, Sue Ann is a full-time RVer, a contributor to Winnebago's WinnebaGoLife blog, and a sought-after motivational speaker.

You can follow along on Sue Ann's travels at:
https://patreon.com/Sueannjaffarian

Works of fiction by Sue Ann Jaffarian include:

DEAD WOMAN DRIVING SERIAL NOVEL
Episode 1: Dead In The Desert
Episode 2: Raising The Dead
Episode 3: Dog Days
Episode 4: Snake Eyes
Episode 5: Haunting the Dead
Episode 6: Married to Death
Episode 7: The Last Death
Episode 8: Sweaty Money
Episode 9: Sweet Scent of Death
Episode 10: Shattered Security (coming soon)

THE ODELIA GREY MYSTERY SERIES
NOVELS
Too Big to Miss

The Curse of the Holy Pail
Thugs and Kisses
Booby Trap
Corpse on the Cob
Twice As Dead
Hide & Snoop
Secondhand Stiff
Hell On Wheels
A Body to Spare
Rhythm & Clues
Too Big To Die

ODELIA GREY SHORT STORIES
Ho Ho Humbug

THE GHOST OF GRANNY APPLES MYSTERY
SERIES
NOVELS
Ghost à la Mode
The Ghost in the Polka Dot Bikini
Gem of a Ghost
Ghost of a Gamble
Ghost in the Guacamole
The Ghosts of Misty Hollow

GRANNY APPLES NOVELLAS
The Silent Ghost
Dummy of a Ghost
The Ghost of Mistletoe Mary
Ghosts 'n Graveyards
The Ghost of Christmas Granny
Ghost Overboard (coming soon)

THE ZELDA BOWEN NOVELS
Finding Zelda
Zelda Doubles Down (coming soon)

THE MADISON ROSE VAMPIRE MYSTERIES
Murder In Vein
Baited Blood

THE WINNIE WILDE ROMANCE SERIES
Running Wilde
Wilde Women
Wilde In Love

OTHER SHORT FICTION
Love Bytes
Early Retirement
Sh*t I'd Kill For

ABOUT THE PUBLISHER

Harbor Lane Books, LLC is a US-based independent, digital publisher of commercial fiction, non-fiction, and poetry.

Connect with Harbor Lane Books on their website www.harborlanebooks.com and TikTok, Instagram, Facebook, Twitter, and Pinterest @harborlanebooks.

Printed in the USA
CPSIA information can be obtained
at www.ICGtesting.com
CBHW061138040624
9550CB00020B/97

9 781963 705966